DON CARTER'S 10 SECRETS of BOWLING

Don Carter's

10 SECRETS of BOWLING

Illustrated by
Anthony Ravielli

NEW YORK · THE VIKING PRESS

PUBLISHED IN 1958 BY THE VIKING PRESS, INC.
625 MADISON AVENUE, NEW YORK 22, N.Y.

REVISED EDITION ISSUED IN 1963

PUBLISHED IN CANADA BY
THE MACMILLAN COMPANY OF CANADA LIMITED

Acknowledgment is made to *Sports Illustrated,* in which a shorter version of this book originally appeared, including a number of the illustrations.

LIBRARY OF CONGRESS CATALOGUE CARD NUMBER:
58-12376
PRINTED IN THE UNITED STATES OF AMERICA

ACKNOWLEDGMENT

I am grateful to the Brunswick Corporation for their cooperation in the preparation of this book and for supplying information about the history and the equipment of bowling.

— Don Carter

Contents

Foreword

In August 1957 when Jerome Snyder, the art editor of *Sports Illustrated,* asked me to illustrate an article about Don Carter and the fundamentals of bowling, I thought it would be a simple assignment. What is there to say, I asked myself, that the average bowler does not already know?

Don and I met at the Roselle bowling lanes in Roselle, New Jersey, to work out the details. As I drove to New Jersey, armed with high-speed cameras, sketchbook, and writing pad, I fully expected to be back at my studio in two or three hours with all the information I needed. *Sports Illustrated* had allotted me four pages for the article and I suspected that I would have to do considerable padding to fill this space.

Don Carter quickly dispelled these naïve notions. We worked continuously for ten hours at the Roselle bowling lanes plus an additional five hours at the Roxy lanes in New York City. Don repeated his delivery several hundred times while I made notes and diagrams, drew rough sketches, and took countless high-speed photographs to make sure I had an accurate record of every phase. There was not a motion in Don's delivery, from stance to release, that did not have a definite, carefully calculated purpose. Listening to his explanations was like listening to a rocket scientist explaining the workings of a guided missile.

André Laguerre, assistant managing editor of *Sports Illustrated,* was so impressed with Don's scientific approach to bowling that he gave me seventeen pages instead of four, and even then the space was not sufficient. This book is an attempt to do full justice for the first time to Don's revolutionary bowling technique. It is the only complete and authoritative exposition that Don has made available apart from personal instruction.

Don Carter's delivery departs in so many ways from accepted methods that many experts first dismissed it as a whimsical eccentricity, failing completely to comprehend its scientific basis. Like all great innovators, Don had to steel himself against early ridicule and prove his principles by performance. His record speaks for itself. Since 1950 he has won every important bowling title, including the first world invitation match championship, held in Chicago in 1957.

To traditionalists, Don's delivery seems strange, but in fact it is simply a streamlined version of the classic bowling style. Much of the violent action in bowling methods developed in past decades, Don has discovered, has a tendency to increase fatigue and lessen efficiency. The accurate, highly polished lanes of today do not require fast balls and strong hooks. Don shuffles casually toward the foul line. He places the ball easily and effortlessly on the lane, and it rolls with moderate speed toward the pins. Then, miraculously, all the pins fall over!

This book will tell you, as best Don and I can, exactly how to do it and why it happens.

—Anthony Ravielli

DON CARTER'S 10 SECRETS of BOWLING

Bowling is one of the oldest of man's pastimes. Before the dawn of history, cave men probably tried to bowl over rows of pointed rocks with rounded stones.

The Story of Bowling

The rolling of a ball toward a standing object, with the avowed intention of bowling it over, is one of the oldest of man's pastimes. Before the dawn of history, cave men probably set up rows of pointed stones and tried to bowl them over with rounded rocks. There is a gruesome legend that ancient savage tribes bowled at upright thigh bones with the skulls of vanquished enemies, using the eye sockets for thumb and finger grips. Sir Flinders Petrie, the great British archaeologist, found the implements for a game very similar to modern tenpins in an Egyptian child's grave which he dated 5200 B.C.

The English game of "bowling on the green" originated in the thirteenth century, but it has more in common with the Italian game of *boccie* than with modern bowling. True, large balls are rolled down lanes of grass toward the "jack" (a peg, cone, or smaller ball), but the purpose is to bowl as close to the jack as possible rather than to knock it over. This form of bowling became enormously popular in England during the fourteenth century; King Edward III was so afraid it might supplant archery, which had important military value, that he forbade the sport, but it continued to flourish on a kind of bootleg basis as a popular form of gambling. Public laws against it continued long after the bow and arrow had been made obsolete by the invention of gunpowder. Today bowling on the green is the national warm-weather sport of Scotland and continues to be one of England's most widely played outdoor games.

Modern bowling, or tenpins, had its origin four centuries ago in Germany and Holland. Martin Luther was so fond of the game that, it is said, he built a private bowling alley for himself and his family. The game was then played (and still is today in Germany) with nine pins, instead of ten, arranged in diamond formation. This game of *Kegelspiel* (bowlers today are still called "keglers") was brought to the United States by the early Dutch settlers of New Amsterdam, now the city of New York. It was played on the green, and until 1840 the most popular gaming area was just north of the Battery where a small park still bears the name of Bowling Green. Remember the story of Rip Van Winkle? The superstitious Dutch settlers, when they heard summer thunder, thought it was the sound of ninepins being played in the Catskills by the ghosts of Henry Hudson and his crew.

In the early part of the nineteenth century the game was surrounded by so much gambling and racketeering that laws against it were passed in New York, Connecticut, and Massachusetts. But citizens soon evaded these laws by adding one more pin and changing the formation from a diamond to the familiar triangle used today. By the middle of the century, basement rooms for playing the "new" game of tenpins could be found in almost every block along Broadway from Fulton to Fourteenth Street. Johnny Cleveland, better known as Tenpin Johnny, was the most famous of the early Broadway champions.

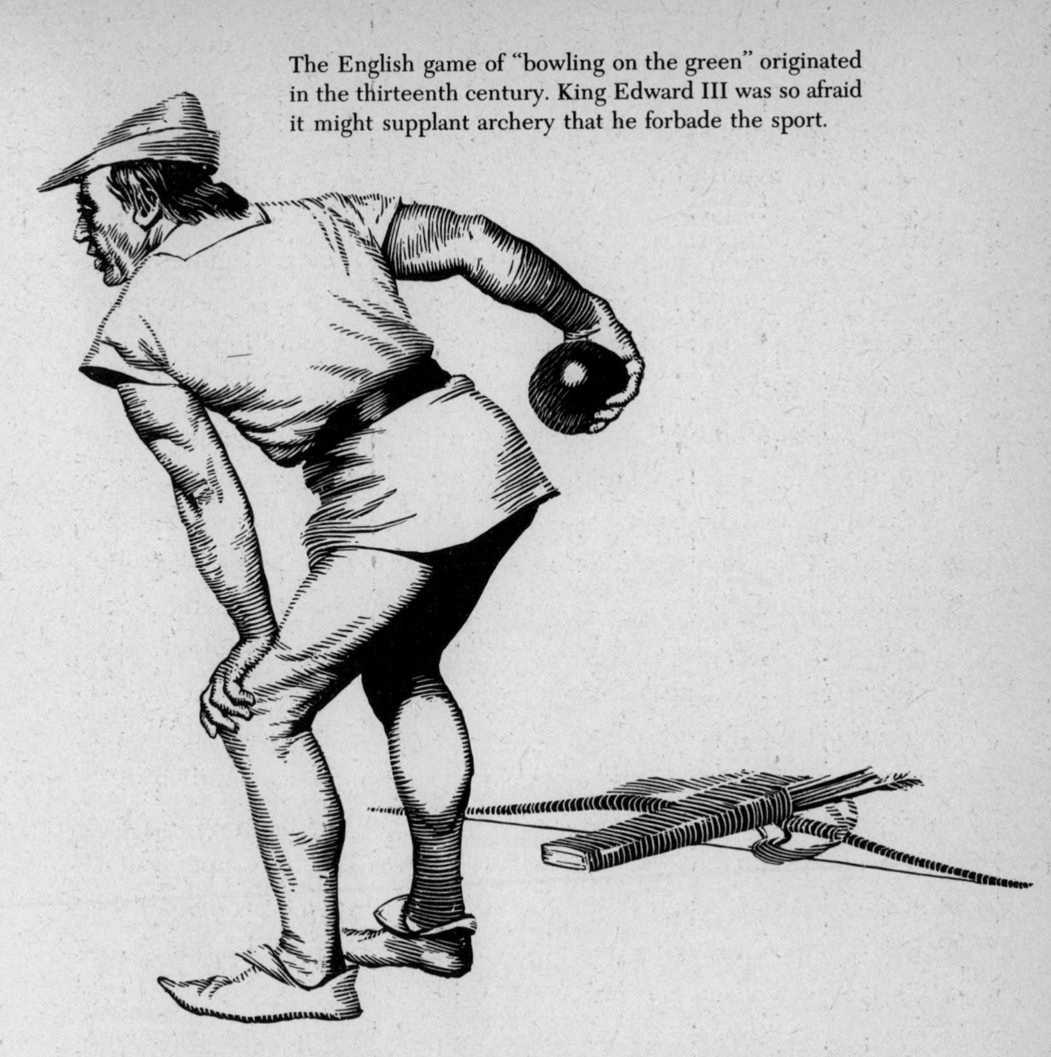
The English game of "bowling on the green" originated in the thirteenth century. King Edward III was so afraid it might supplant archery that he forbade the sport.

In those days bowling establishments were called "bowling saloons." The word saloon, a corruption of the French word *salon,* was applied to all sorts of places—ice-cream saloons, shaving saloons, billiard saloons, whisky saloons—to suggest a refined air of fashion and grandeur. Toward the end of the century, larger bowling rooms would be found at various "Palaces of Fun and Amusement," alongside the skating rink, dance hall, and penny arcade.

There was a distressing lack of uniformity in bowling rules and equipment until 1875. All sizes of lanes, balls, and pins were in use, and a man who learned to bowl a good game at one saloon might be a poor player if he went across the street to another. It was in 1875 that the first attempt was made to set up standards. Twenty-seven delegates from nine bowling clubs of Manhattan and Brooklyn met in Germania Hall, in the Bowery, to organize the short-lived National Bowling Association. This group decided that sixty feet would be the official distance from the center of the head-pin to the bowler's foul line, a distance that remains standard today. It had previously varied from fifty to a hundred feet, depending on the length of the room. The Association also set standard dimensions for the pins, but present-day pins are slightly smaller than those in use then.

In New York City twenty years later, on September 9, 1895, the American Bowling Congress was organized to enforce corrective measures against gambling excesses and to refine further the rules and regulations. Henry Timm, Joe Thum, Louis Stein, H. Feldman, and Sam Karpf were among the great bowlers of the time who attended the organizing convention at Beethoven Hall. Today the ABC, with headquarters in Milwaukee, is the parent governing body of the sport in the United States and Canada.

At the turn of the century there were approximately fifteen thousand bowlers in the country and some four hundred and fifty public establishments. As the nation's population grew, interest in the game grew even faster. By 1920 there were a million bowlers in the United States, two thousand establishments averaging three or four lanes each, and about five hundred annual tournaments for men sponsored by the ABC. Today there are more than twenty million bowlers and about eleven thousand establishments.

When you compare the modern bowling center with a typical bowling saloon that your grandfather may have frequented fifty years ago, you get a vivid impression of how rapidly interest in the sport has grown. The saloon, with one or two alleys, would be in a damp, dimly lit, badly ventilated basement that reeked of cigar smoke and stale beer. Lopsided wooden balls would wobble down a warped lane to the accompaniment of violent cursing. No respectable woman or child would think of entering the place. A sleepy pin boy would call out the number of pins knocked down, leisurely set the pins back in approximately correct formation,

Modern bowling was brought to the United States by the early Dutch settlers. The game was then played with nine pins instead of ten.

then return the ball on a rickety sloping rail.

Now let's take a look inside one of the modern bowling centers that have recently been built in California. The first impression is one of sumptuous splendor. You enter through a luxurious lobby lined with sofas and easy chairs. You walk across plush carpets, listening to soft music from concealed loudspeakers. There may be a restaurant and a cocktail lounge on the premises. Rest rooms are large and clean. A nursery for the youngsters is supervised by a registered nurse. If it is mid-summer, the center is air-conditioned. Inside the huge bowling hall itself there are fifty lanes or more and not a single pin boy. The pins are picked up and set accurately in place by ingenious automatic pin-setting machines. Your score is flashed on a screen above the lane.

Take a look at the players. There are almost as many women as men, almost as many children as adults. It is not surprising to see a six-year-old boy rolling the balls with his seventy-year-old grandmother. Physically handicapped persons also have found bowling a stimulating sport, including even the blind, who use a special "range finder" devised by the Brunswick-Balke-Collender Company, the nation's leading manufacturer of bowling equipment.

Today in the United States, where bowling is more popular than in any other country, it has become an all-year-round, all-family game. It was during the Second World War that women started flocking to the lanes in large numbers. Annual tournaments for the ladies are now sponsored by the Women's International Bowling Congress (founded in 1916), and scores of lady bowlers of all ages are among the nation's top players. Mrs. Marion Ladewig, an attractive, trim-figured grandmother, of Grand Rapids, Michigan, is the present United States women's champion and perhaps the greatest woman bowler of all time.

Increasing numbers of teen-agers also are taking up the sport, and many high schools have their own bowling leagues, which

At the turn of the century bowling establishments were called "saloons" and were regarded as disreputable by the more respectable people of that era.

compete with leagues of other schools. The American Junior Bowling Congress (organized in 1935) sponsors separate leagues for boys and girls, does not permit smoking during league play, and prohibits competition in establishments where a bar is open during the time of play. Of course many colleges also stress bowling as a sport and in some cases provide credit in physical education for the participants.

The most spectacular area of growth in bowling popularity since World War II has been in the field of industrial recreation.

It is not unusual for a large corporation to sponsor as many as five hundred bowling teams as part of its recreation program for employees from the boss down to the office boy. Before the war these industrial teams were usually all men or all women. In recent years, however, the mixed team has been gaining favor rapidly as more and more girls take up the game and find, to their everlasting delight, that it is one sport in which it is possible for them to give their male office associates a good trouncing.

What about the future of the sport? Every year more and more Americans are discovering that bowling is an ideal combination of not too strenuous physical exercise, mental relaxation, and friendly social contacts. The game also is growing in popularity in other nations, especially in Japan and the Scandinavian countries. In 1957 at Chicago I had the honor of winning the world's first international bowling tournament.

Bowling has come a long way from its humble beginning as the German game of ninepins. Today bowling is enjoyed by more Americans than take part in any other participant sport with the possible exception of fishing. This enjoyment includes watching bowling tournaments as well as playing in them, for in the last few years the television networks have discovered that a bowling match can be an exciting, dramatic event on the screen. The old aura of disrepute is completely gone. Bowling has become as fashionable as tennis was in the twenties. And I think it is safe to say that its world-wide growth as a family sport is just beginning.

The Secrets of Bowling

It was in 1948, when I was 20, that I decided to give up professional baseball (I was pitching for one of the Philadelphia Athletics' farm clubs) and take up bowling in earnest. It had long been one of my favorite sports. I had admired the smooth delivery of many bowling stars, Ned Day in particular, but I resolved not to imitate them. Instead I asked myself: how can one reduce the delivery of the ball to its absolute essentials?

This book is the outcome of ten years of thought and experimentation given to this question. I do not say that my "system" is best for every player. A player who has developed a style of his own would be unwise to make radical changes. But I do believe that champions in all sports owe their success to having stripped their style, as I have done, to bedrock fundamentals.

The most revolutionary aspect of my style—and the most misunderstood—is my technique of keeping the right arm bent throughout the swing. Some people think that a physical defect prevents me from straightening the arm. To others I give the impression of trying to "push" the ball down the lane. When I first began practicing this method, experts raised their eyebrows in astonishment. But two years later, when I became National Individual Match champion, they began to take my style more seriously. One bowling instructor who had laughed the hardest at "Push-Ball Carter" in 1952 is today teaching the bent-arm method.

Why do I bend my arm? Let me answer this with another question. If an engineer were to design a mechanical arm for rolling a heavy ball accurately toward a target, would he design it with a central hinge? Obviously not. A flexible middle joint would be wholly uncalled for. By keeping my elbow locked and my shoulder free, I create a rigid pendulum that swings the ball in the simplest possible way. I used to practice it in my cellar by swinging a heavy clothes iron. For months there was no noticeable improvement in my game. Then suddenly I got the "feel" of the new method and it began to pay off handsome dividends.

Another basic secret of my style is this. I have not diffused my efforts by learning different types of delivery for different types of spares. As you will see in the section of this book devoted to the second ball, I use exactly the same delivery on every occasion. As a result, all my experience has been concentrated on the perfection of one thing—a simplified pendulum delivery of the ball.

On the following pages I have broken down the technique of this delivery into ten basic steps, beginning with the method by which I grip the ball.

To avoid having his fingers smashed by a returning ball, the player should always take the ball from the rack with his hands on the sides, as shown here.

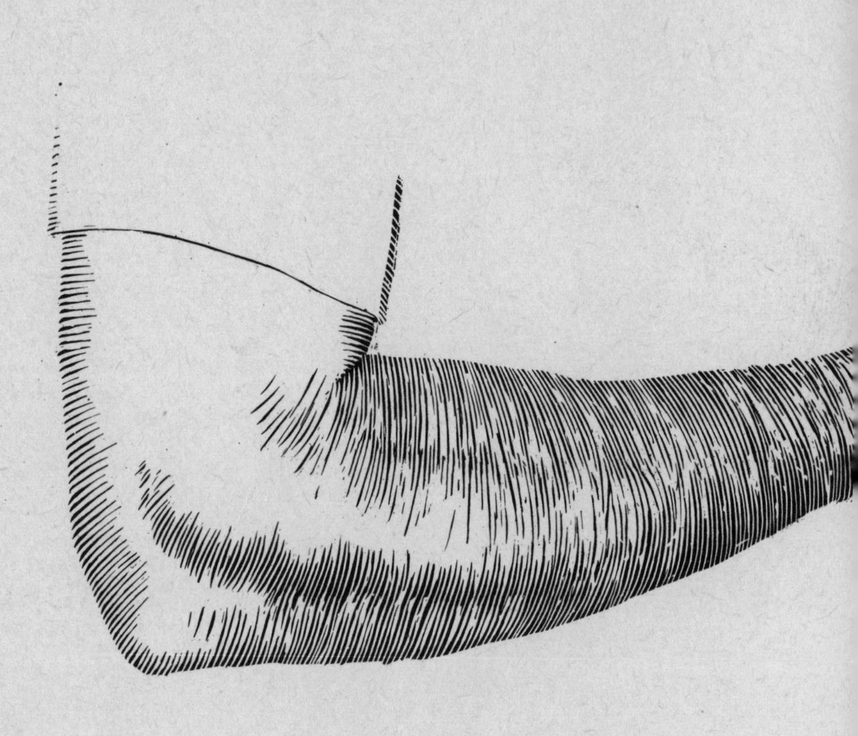

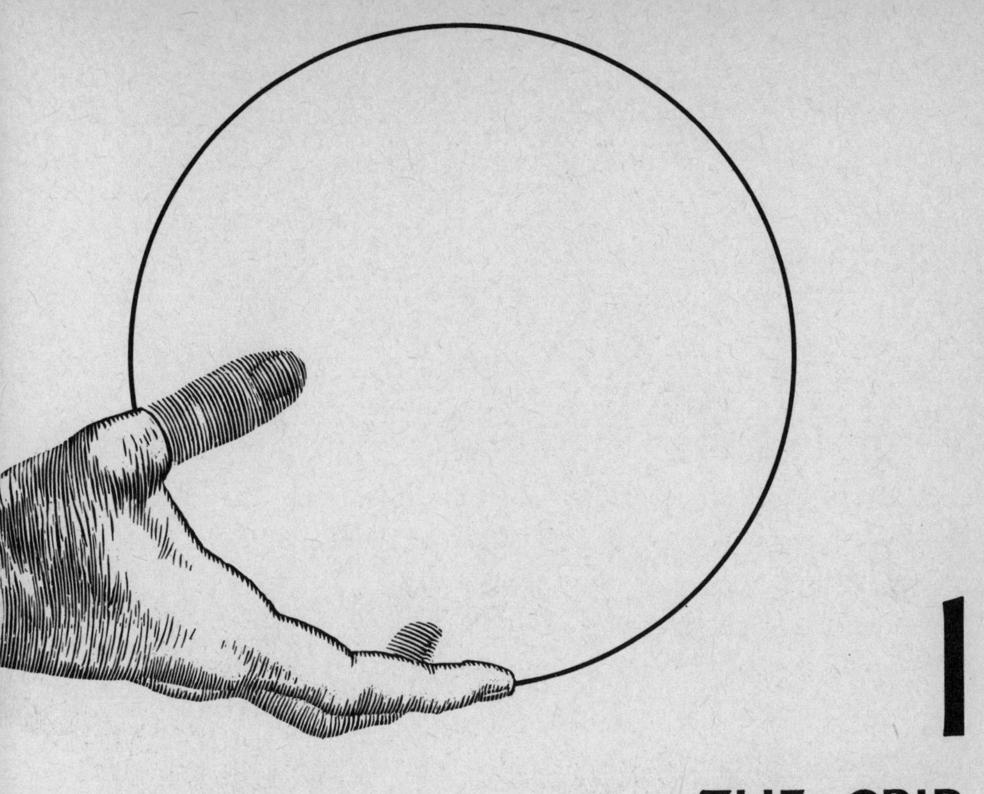

1
THE GRIP

Bowling balls range in weight from nine to sixteen pounds and vary in the arrangement of finger and thumb holes. A beginner should select a ball that he can grip and swing without strain. A lighter ball is easier to handle at first; later he can gradually work up to a heavier ball that kicks up a bigger "storm" when it hits the pins. Experts use a variety of grips, some quite unusual. The three-finger grip I use is illustrated on the next two pages.

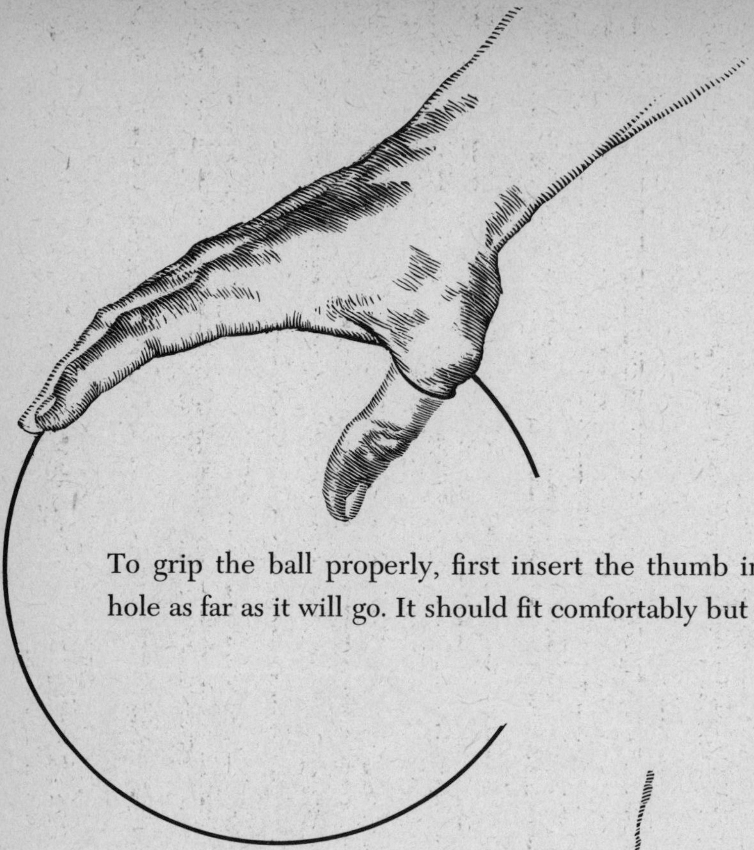

To grip the ball properly, first insert the thumb into the thumb hole as far as it will go. It should fit comfortably but not too snugly.

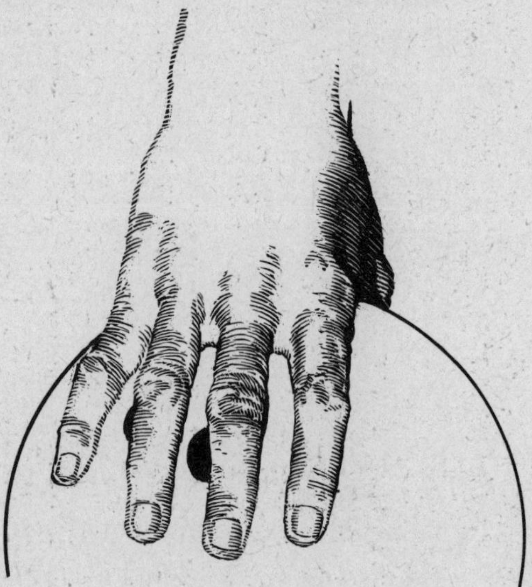

Let your fingers rest naturally on the ball. The span between the thumb hole and the finger holes should be such that the middle joints of the second and third fingers extend to the front edge of the finger holes.

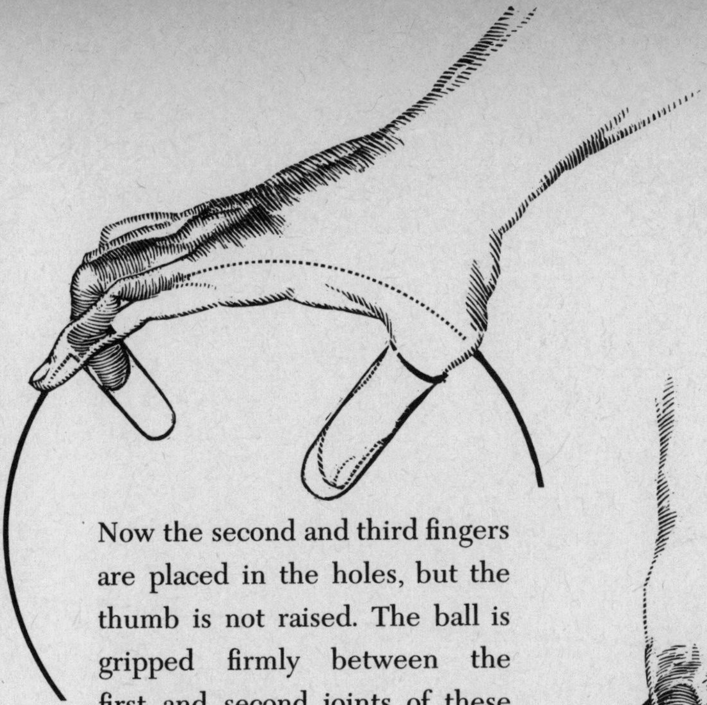

Now the second and third fingers are placed in the holes, but the thumb is not raised. The ball is gripped firmly between the first and second joints of these two fingers.

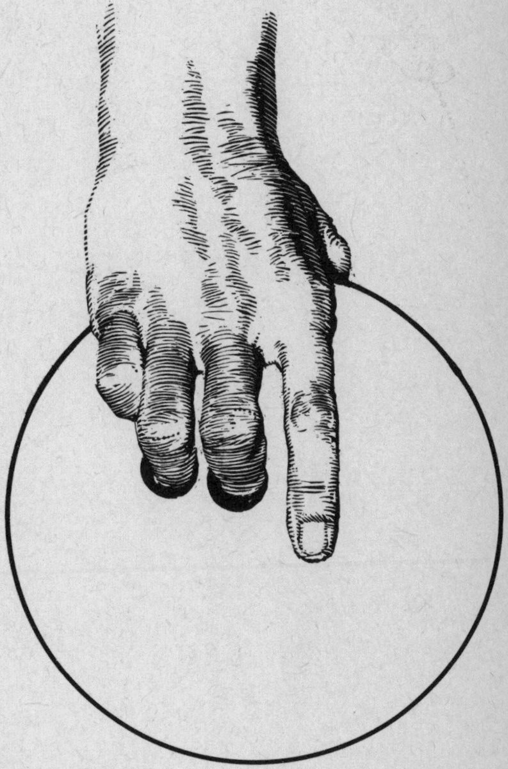

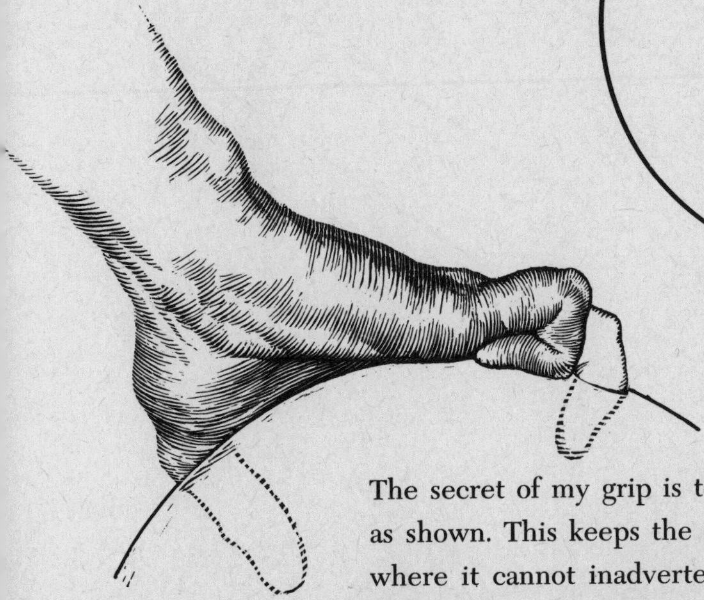

The secret of my grip is to curl my little finger as shown. This keeps the finger out of the way, where it cannot inadvertently twist the ball. It also uses the curled finger as a cushion to relieve strain on the other fingers.

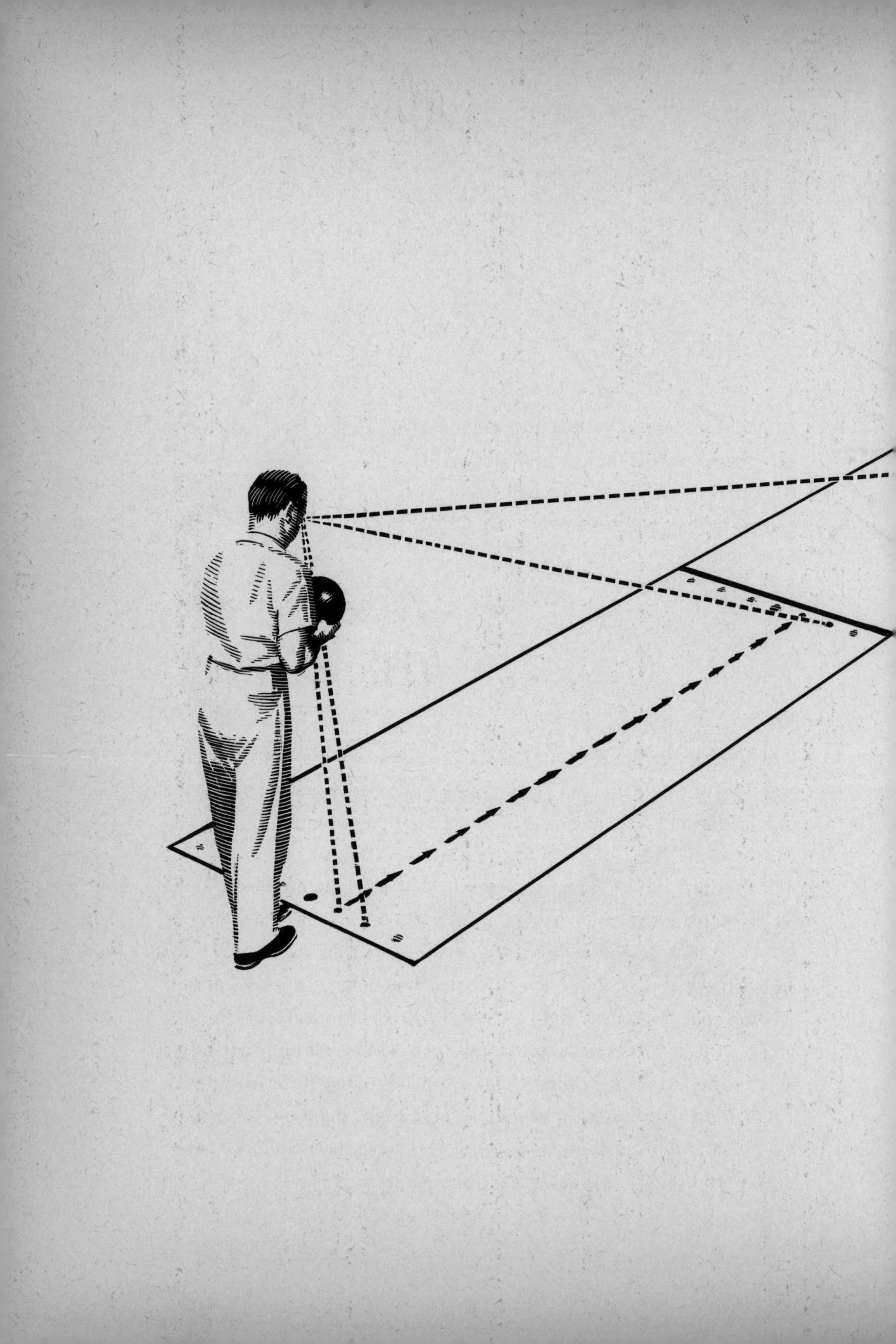

2

THE STANCE

It is during the stance, or starting position, that the player takes aim. The "target" may be on the pins, a board along which he plans to roll the ball, a marker on the lane, or a combination of various check points. The spot method is preferred by most experts. I fix my attention on the second spot from the right on the row of markers (usually arrow-shaped) nearest the pins. This is my target. I stand a foot or two behind the row of dots that are twelve feet in back of the foul line. The ball will leave the foul line at the second spot from the right, which is on the same board as my target. If it crosses the target it will hook to the left and strike the pins in the 1-3 pocket where it is most likely to scatter all of them. Today most lanes are uniformly polished, but if my first ball breaks too much and hits the head pin flush, I will have to move my stance slightly to the left and shoot for the same target.

My stance is upright but relaxed, with the ball held slightly above my waist. My left foot is ahead of the other and pointing directly forward.

My shoulders are parallel with the foul line. Note that my left hand supports the ball. This takes all strain from the right hand, which does nothing more than grip the ball comfortably.

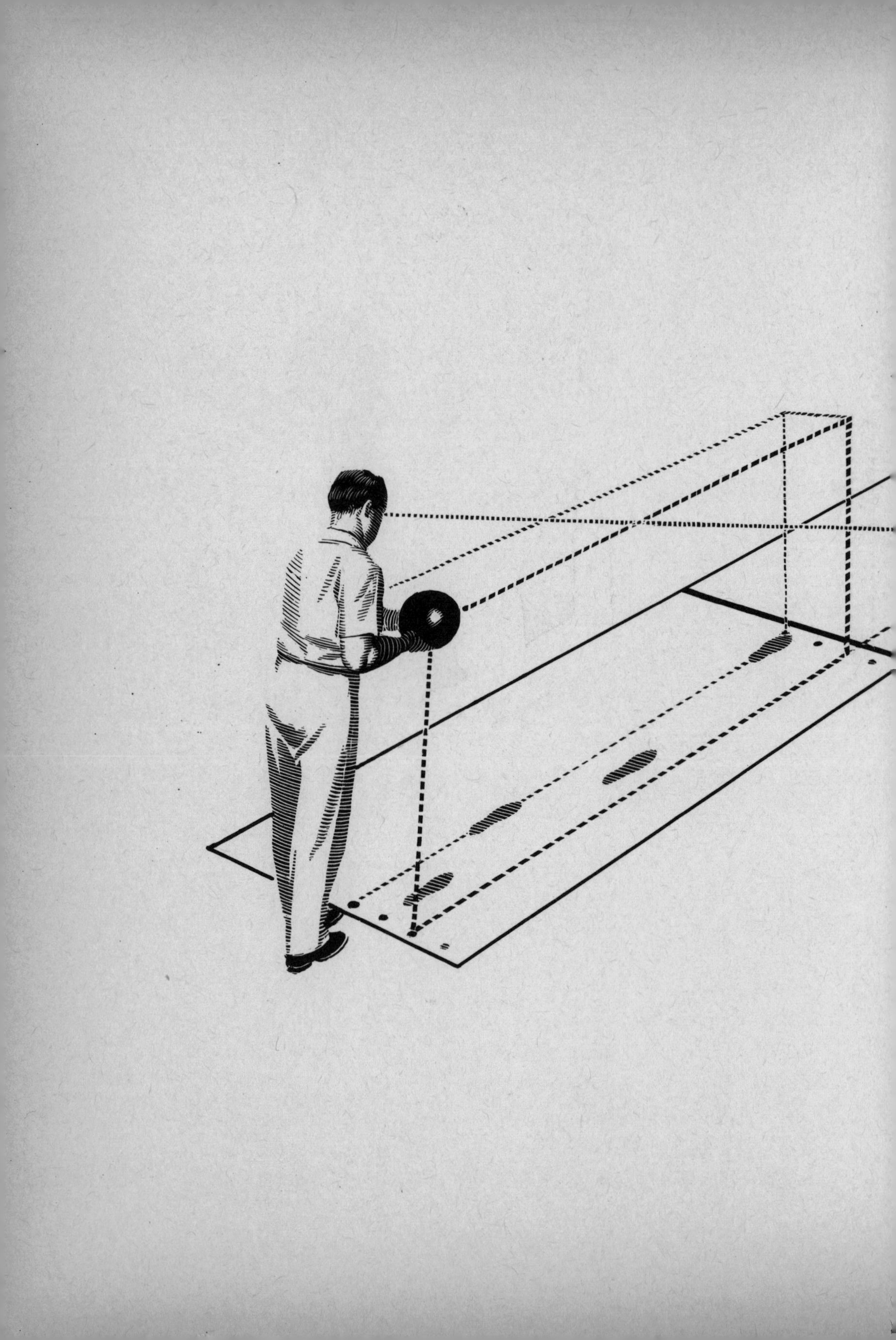

3
THE ADDRESS

This stage, which sets the ball in motion, is extremely important. The ball is heavy, and if you start it moving incorrectly it is almost impossible to correct the error later. The object of my address is to start the ball swinging on an imaginary plane that is perpendicular to the floor and has its lower edge on the board that leads to my target. The next two pages show how this is achieved.

In the illustration on the left I am in the stance position, my weight on the right foot. The next two pictures show how I lift the ball above eye level. Note that my left hand still carries the ball. When the ball reaches its maximum height I shift it to the right.

If I did not do this now I would be forced to do it during the downswing and so lose control, or I would have to contort my body to get out of the ball's way. As the ball is lowered I lean forward slightly, rolling my weight to the left foot.

4

THE FIRST STEP

In approaching the foul line most experts take either four or five steps. Three-steppers are rarely seen today in professional play. I use the four-step delivery. The steps must be in a perfectly straight line. It is at the start of the first, as my right foot reaches out, that I simultaneously push the ball away. This action is a smooth, coordinated move and extremely important to the rhythm of the entire delivery.

THE PUSHAWAY

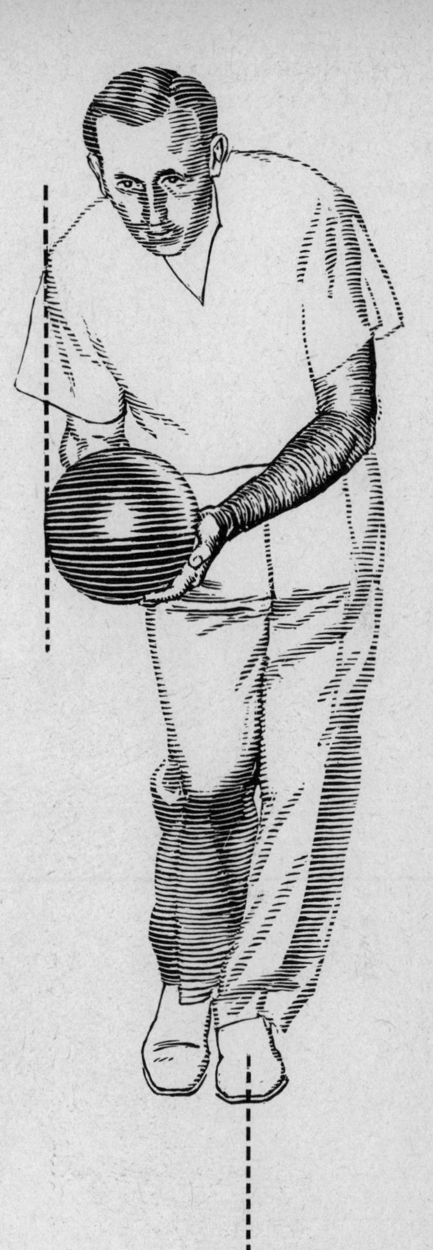

As I start to move forward my right arm is bent at right angles pushing the ball forward along the imaginary plane that intersects the target.

END OF THE FIRST STEP

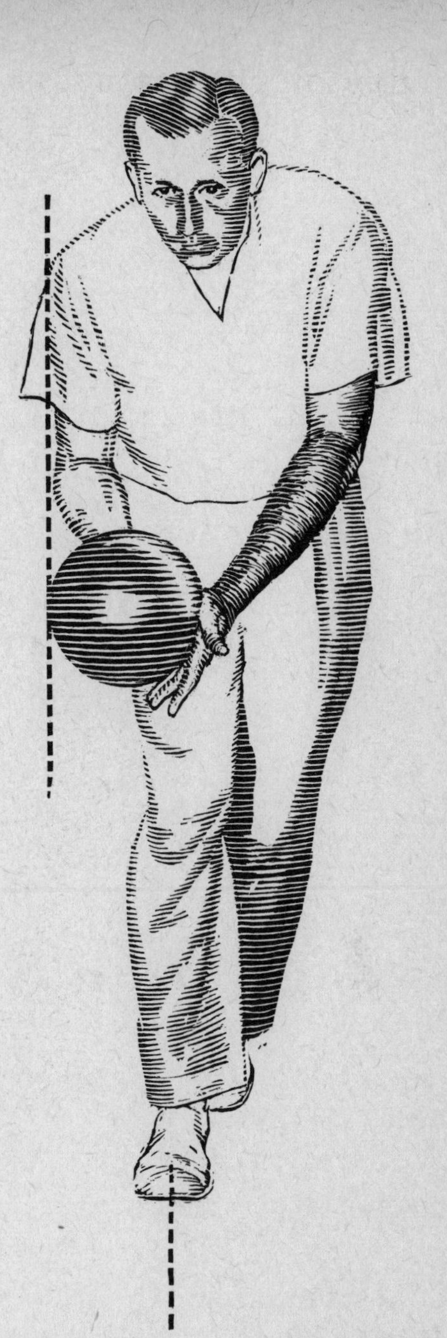

At the end of the step, with the weight now on my right foot, my left hand still partly carries the ball. This helps to push the ball forward and also to keep the ball on its true path.

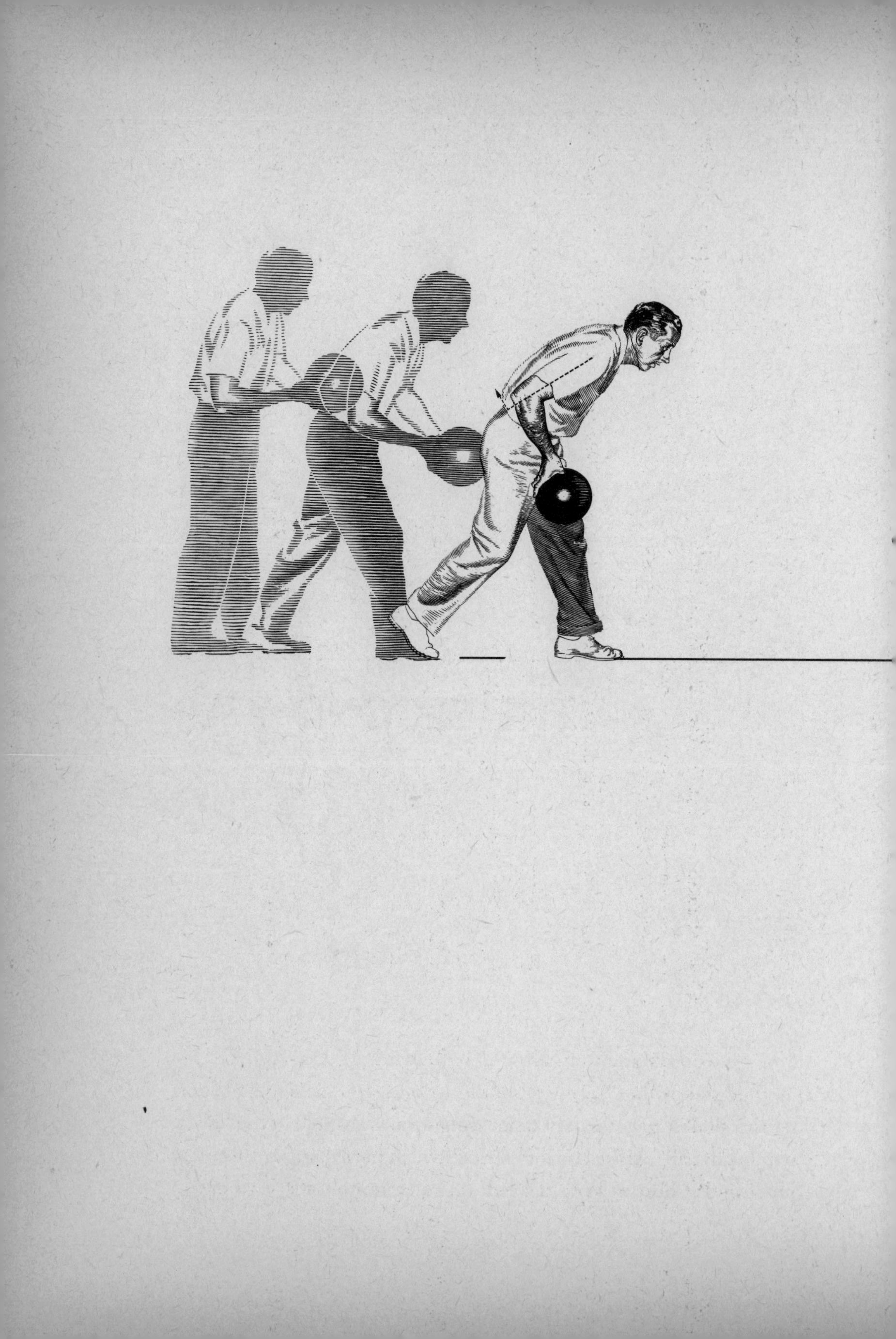

5

THE SECOND STEP

Smooth coordination of arm and footwork is essential to any method of bowling. In my style the second step, which actually is more a shuffling movement than a step, brings the ball to the lowest point of its arc. Most bowlers straighten the arm during this step, but I find it best to keep it bent as shown on the next two pages.

START OF THE SECOND STEP

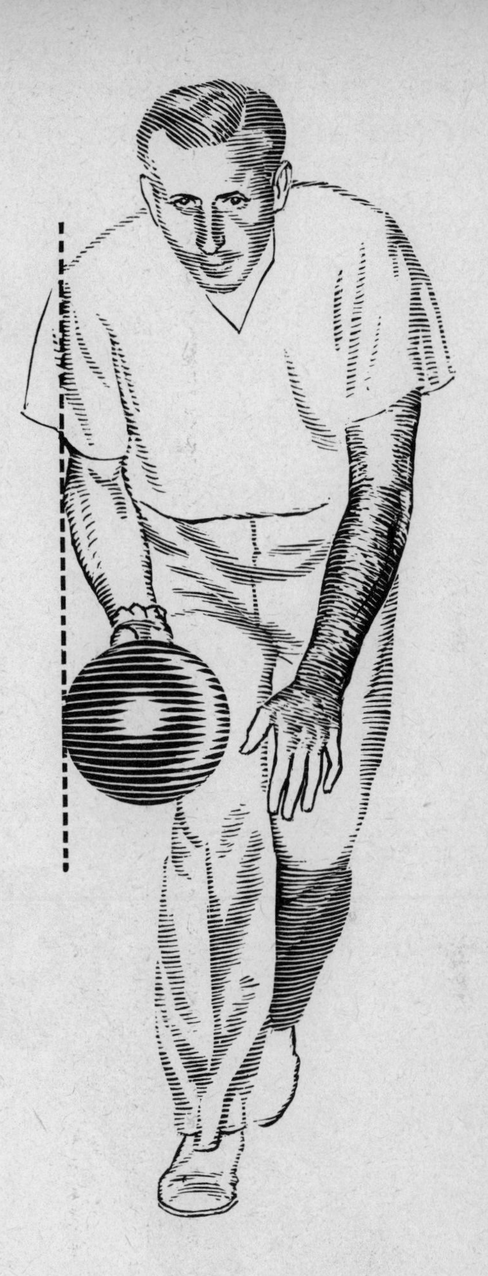

At the start of the second step I release the ball with my left hand just as it starts on its backswing. By keeping my arm bent I maintain better control over the swing.

CONTINUATION
OF THE SECOND STEP

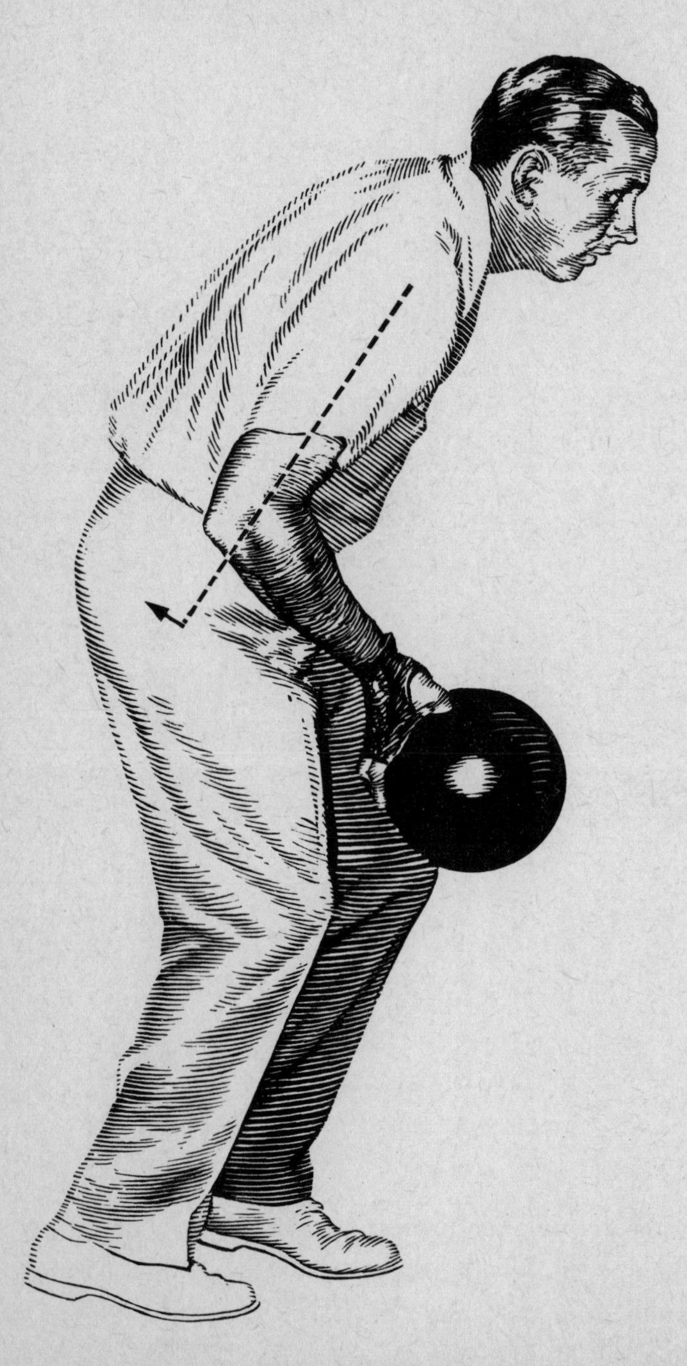

Halfway through the step my left arm has moved to the position shown above. My right arm and wrist are kept firm, forming a kind of right-angled pendulum that swings free at the shoulder.

END OF THE SECOND STEP

The second step ends with the left foot forward. Note that my left arm has swung out to maintain body balance. My "pendulum arm" is unchanged in every respect except that it has swung farther back as my body moves ahead.

6

THE THIRD STEP

This step carries the ball to the top of its backswing. I do not straighten my arm on the backswing, but my technique of keeping it bent has been carefully planned and practiced for many years.

START OF THE THIRD STEP

Until this moment I have been leaning forward only slightly. Now I start to bend my body and at the same time accelerate my speed. My eyes are still glued to the arrow-shaped target. At no time during the delivery do I look at the pins.

END OF THE THIRD STEP

The third step ends with the right foot forward and the ball at the top of its backswing. Note that my right arm is still bent. My wrist has not turned. Even with a straight-arm swing the ball should never go higher than your shoulder. On the other hand, too short a swing will not generate enough speed on the ball.

7

THE FOURTH STEP

Until now the body has been accelerating forward to build up momentum for the ball and power for the final delivery. Now the big moment approaches — the so-called "explosion point" at which this stored-up power will be released.

THE FOURTH STEP
A
B
C

The fourth step begins (A) with the weight on the right foot. The left foot and right arm now move ahead together. The left foot, instead of being raised, is kept on the floor and slid forward (B) on its leather sole, along the same board on which it rested in the stance. As the right foot pushes the body ahead, the weight gradually shifts to the left foot (C). From here on, the right leg is used mainly for balance.

8

SLIDE AND STOP

The final "stop" is usually considered either as the end of the "slide" (fourth step) or the beginning of the "release." It is pictured here as a separate step so that certain vital points, often overlooked, can be made clear.

The slide is made with the weight resting on the *ball* of the left foot. I crouch lower than most bowlers at this point because my right arm is still bent and it is necessary to lower the ball to the lane. As the ball reaches my left foot, I have come to the end of my slide. My left foot remains on the spot on which it stops until the ball is well down the lane. Note how my right leg and left arm are extended leftward to maintain balance.

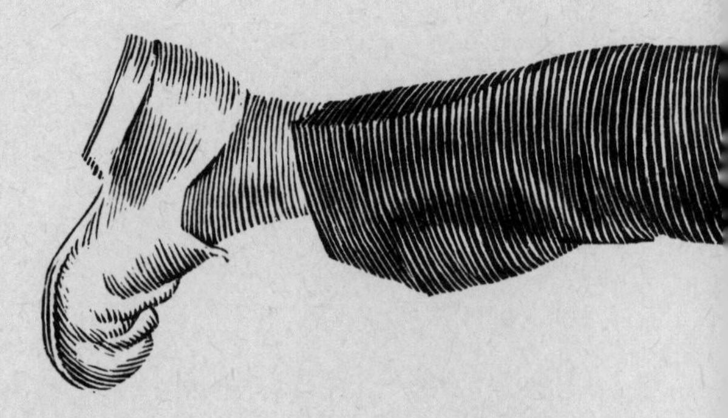

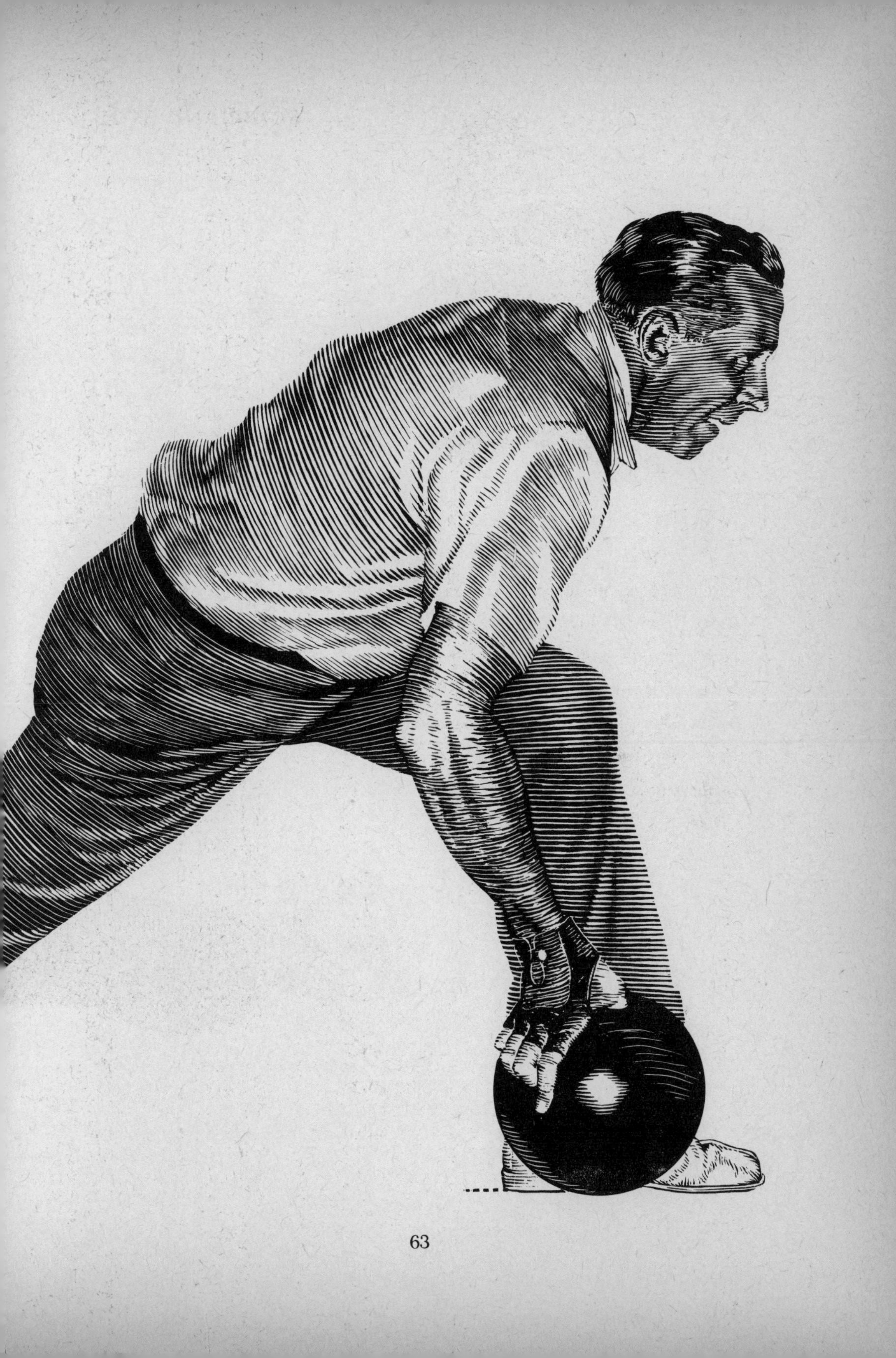

9

THE RELEASE

The climax of the delivery is, of course, the "explosion point" when the ball leaves the hand. From here on the ball is on its own; nothing more can be done to influence its behavior.

THE RELEASE

My left foot has stopped about four inches behind the foul line but my hand has carried the ball well over the line. When I release the ball my thumb comes out first; then I give a slight "lift" to the ball with my fingers. This automatically turns the wrist slightly and gives the ball a moderate "hook." Up until this moment my wrist has been firm (a loose wrist means a wobbly ball during the swing), but now I allow it to turn naturally as I lift the ball. It is not a conscious effort to snap or twist the wrist, such as so many bowlers make to produce a stronger hook. A violent hook is not necessary for high scoring.

This shows in more detail how my hand "lifts" the ball to give it a moderate counter-clockwise spin. The lift automatically turns the wrist about an inch as shown in small pictures A and B.

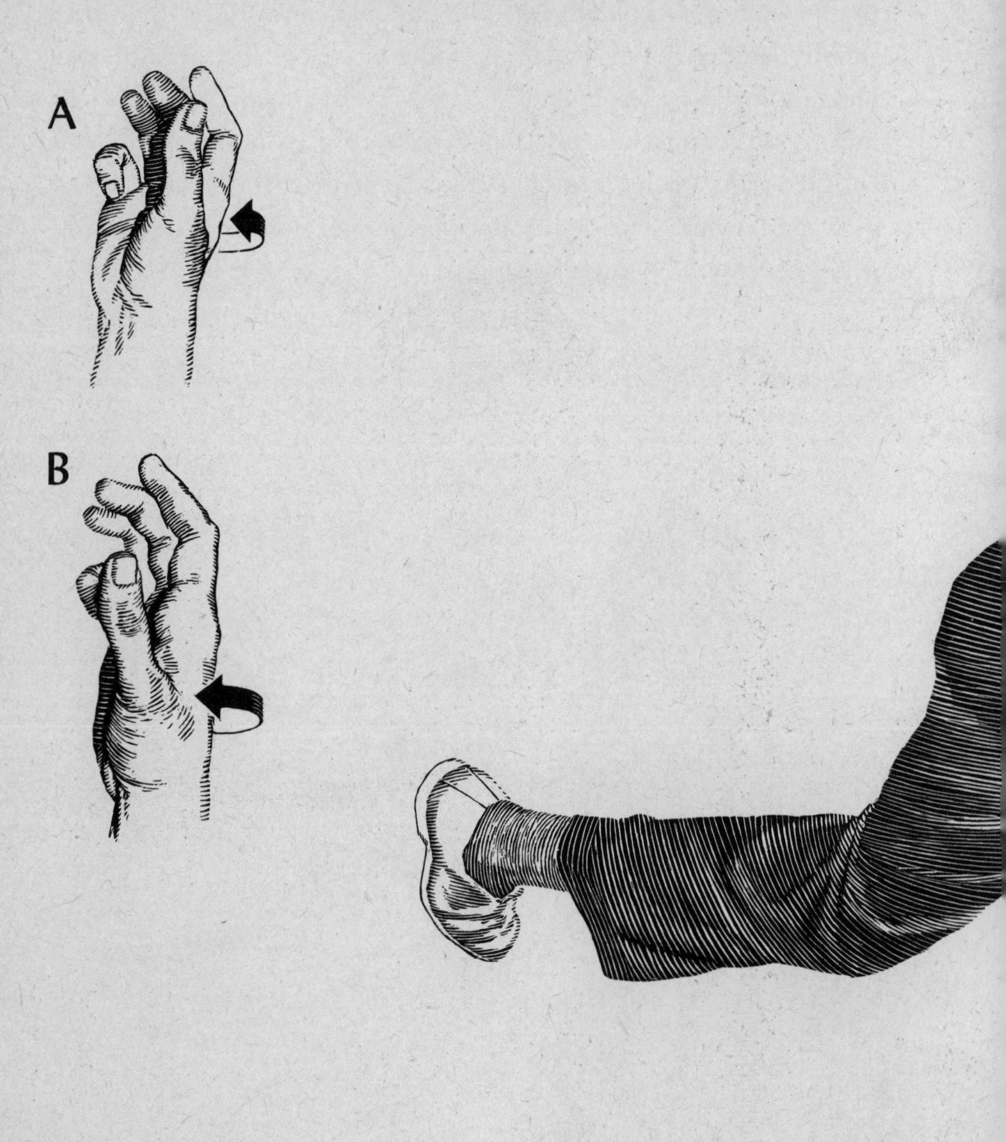

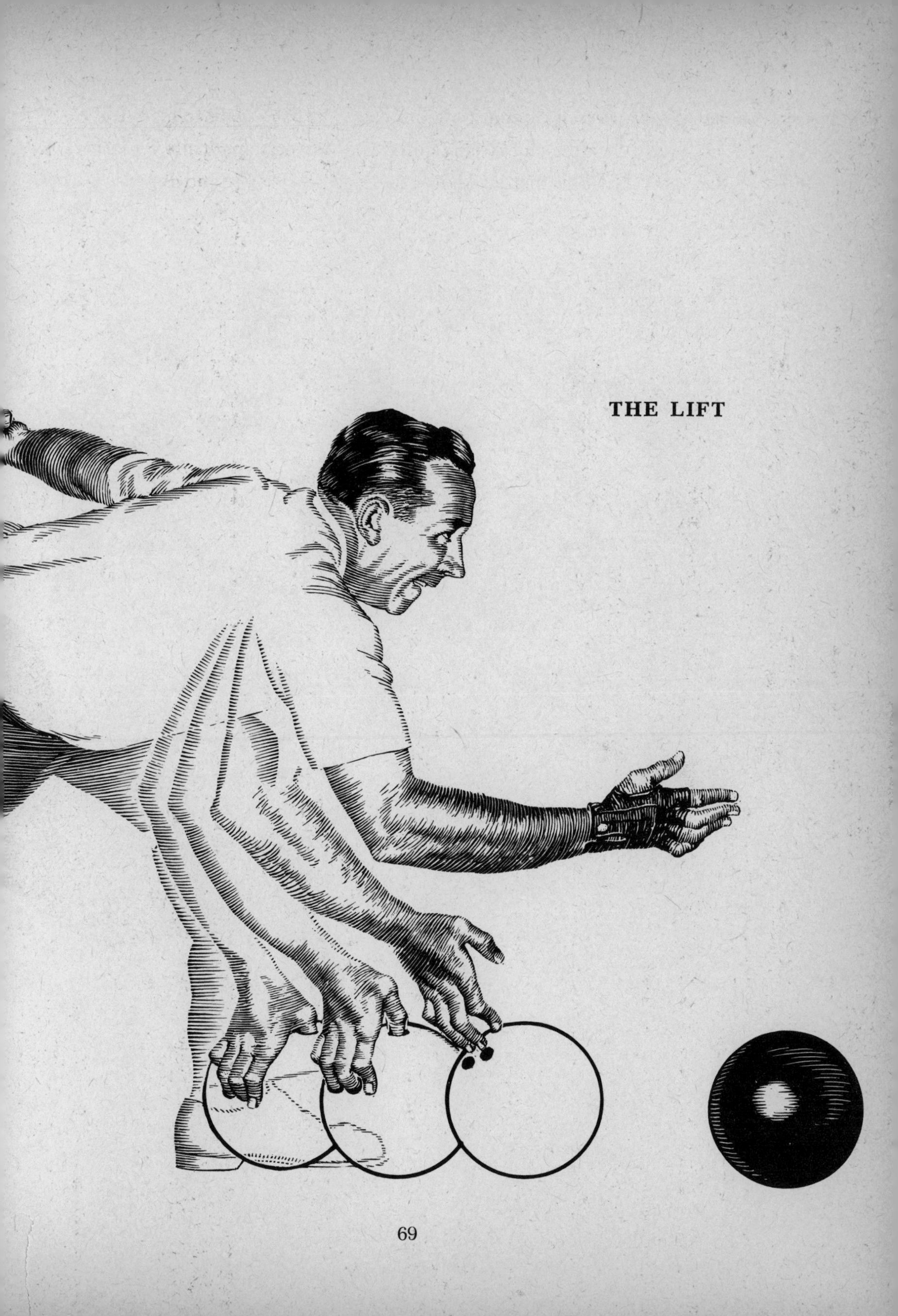

THE LIFT

10
THE FOLLOW-THROUGH

For good bowling form, a delivery is not complete without a full, graceful follow-through that leaves the player perfectly balanced as he watches the progress of his ball toward the pins. Some bowlers follow through by flinging the arm out to the right; others carry it to the left shoulder. I prefer a follow-through that is straight ahead along the perpendicular plane that leads to the target.

My follow-through allows the arm to continue straight forward in the natural arc of its swing. It is important to watch the course of the ball down the lane in order to learn as much as possible for future guidance.

At the end of my follow-through I am in a kind of crouched, one-legged, hand-shaking position, my right leg high in the air. I hold this position until the ball is nearing the pins.

THE FOLLOW-THROUGH

Summary

Although for explanatory purposes I have divided the delivery into ten fundamental steps, actually it is one continuous, co-ordinated motion from stance to follow-through. Regardless of his style, every topnotch kegler repeats his delivery in precisely the same manner every time. Only in this way can he maintain consistently accurate results.

I begin by standing a foot or two behind the twelve-foot mark, my shoulders parallel with the foul line. My body is relaxed and free of all tenseness. My left hand holds the ball waist-high. The little finger is curled to cushion the ball and prevent it from interfering with the ball's release.

I raise the ball above my eyes, then shift it to the right so that my pendulum arm can swing freely on a vertical plane that cuts the target. My target is the second arrow from the right, about sixteen feet down the lane from the foul line. From start to finish my eyes never leave this target.

If you look back over the pictures of the four steps you will see that my feet do not leave the floor until the ball is released. My head is slowly lowered as I move forward. If I took actual steps my head would bob up and down and this would greatly disrupt the smooth arc of the swing. To eliminate this bobbing I shuffle toward the foul line. It is almost as if the ball and I were ballroom-dancing together.

As I move ahead, my bent right arm, with its locked elbow and wrist, swivels freely at the shoulder. It forms a perfect pendulum that carries the ball through the smallest possible arc that will still permit the ball's release on the lane with sufficient force to knock down the pins. A controlled ball moving at a moderate speed is preferable to an exceedingly fast ball which may, at times, slice its way through the pack and keep the pins from mixing.

My "explosion point" occurs at the end of a long slide when the ball has passed my left foot. At this instant I lift the ball slightly with my fingers to give it a moderate hook to the left as it is set on the lane ahead of the foul line. My right arm follows through by continuing straight ahead along its former arc. In this low crouch, with my right leg in the air and to the left, I remain poised as I watch the ball approach the pins.

The firm but freely swinging pendulum, with no waste motion at the elbow, is the key concept of this technique. Any motion of the body that interferes with this natural swing will lower the accuracy of the delivery. Once you have mastered the pendulum swing, the more you practice it the more control you will achieve.

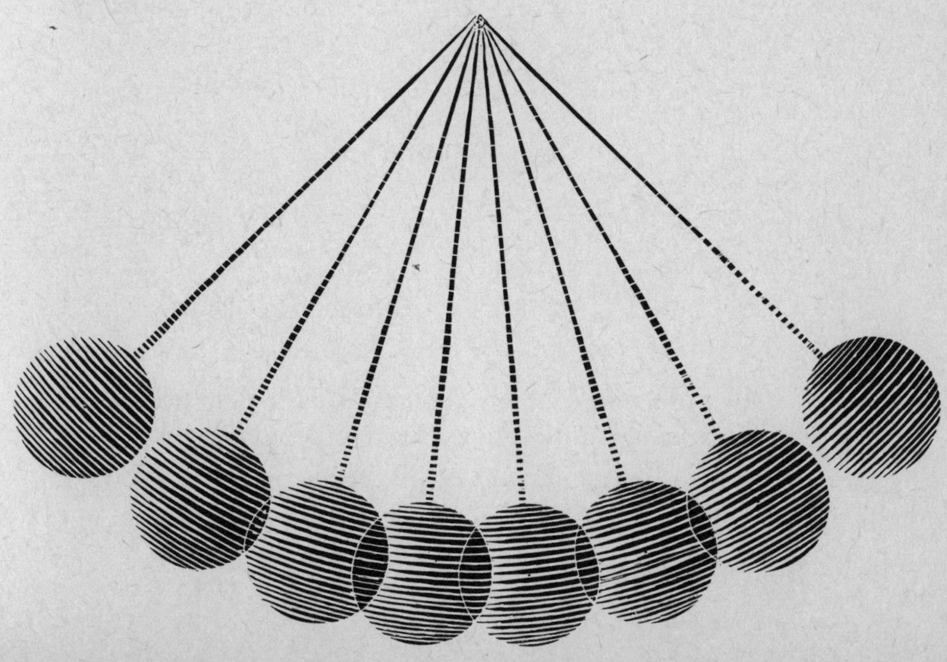

Here is shown exactly how my right arm forms a rigid pendulum that swivels freely at the shoulder. In this way it becomes the closest possible human version of the type of robot bowler that an engineer would design if he eliminated all unnecessary elements from his artificial arm.

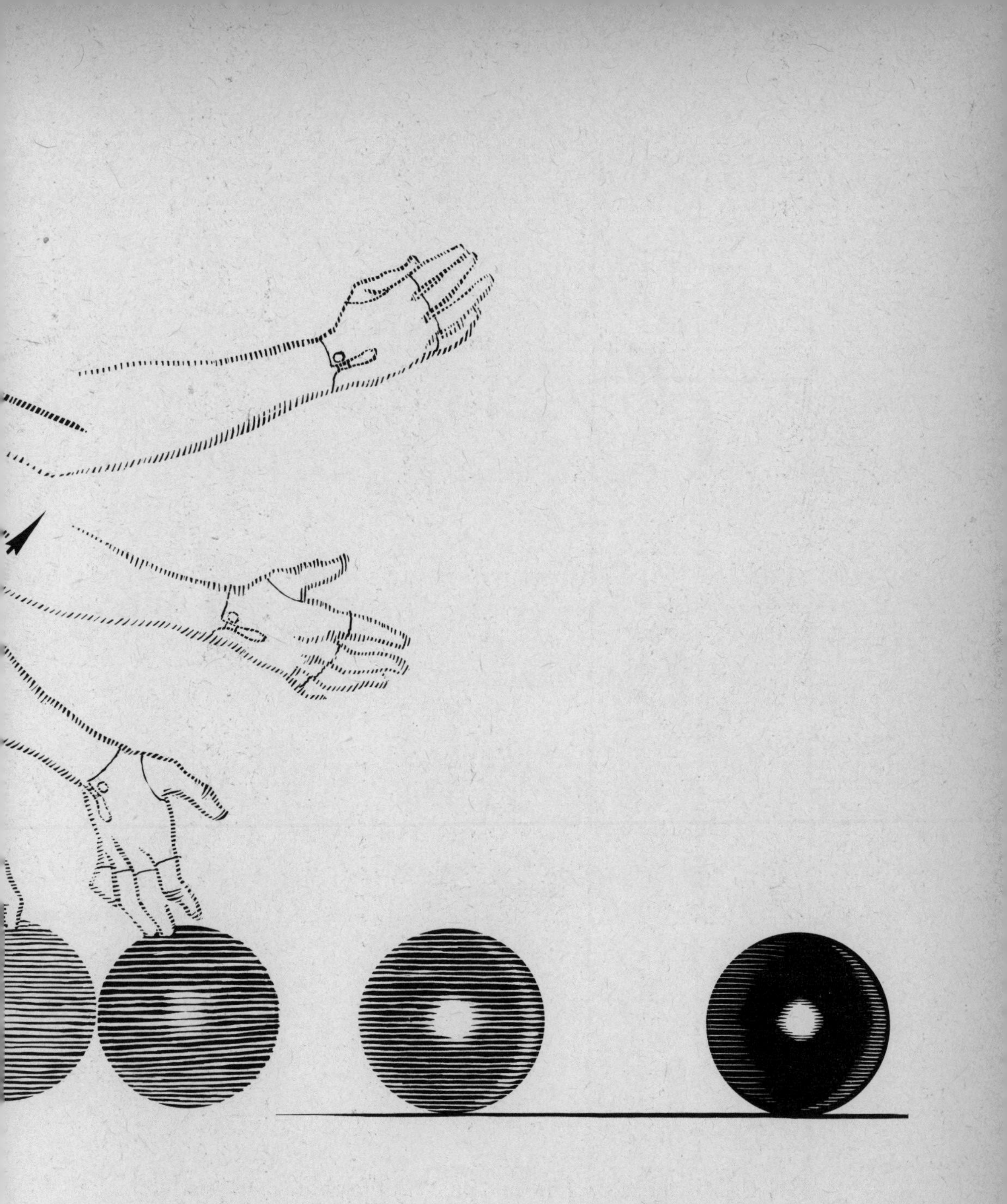

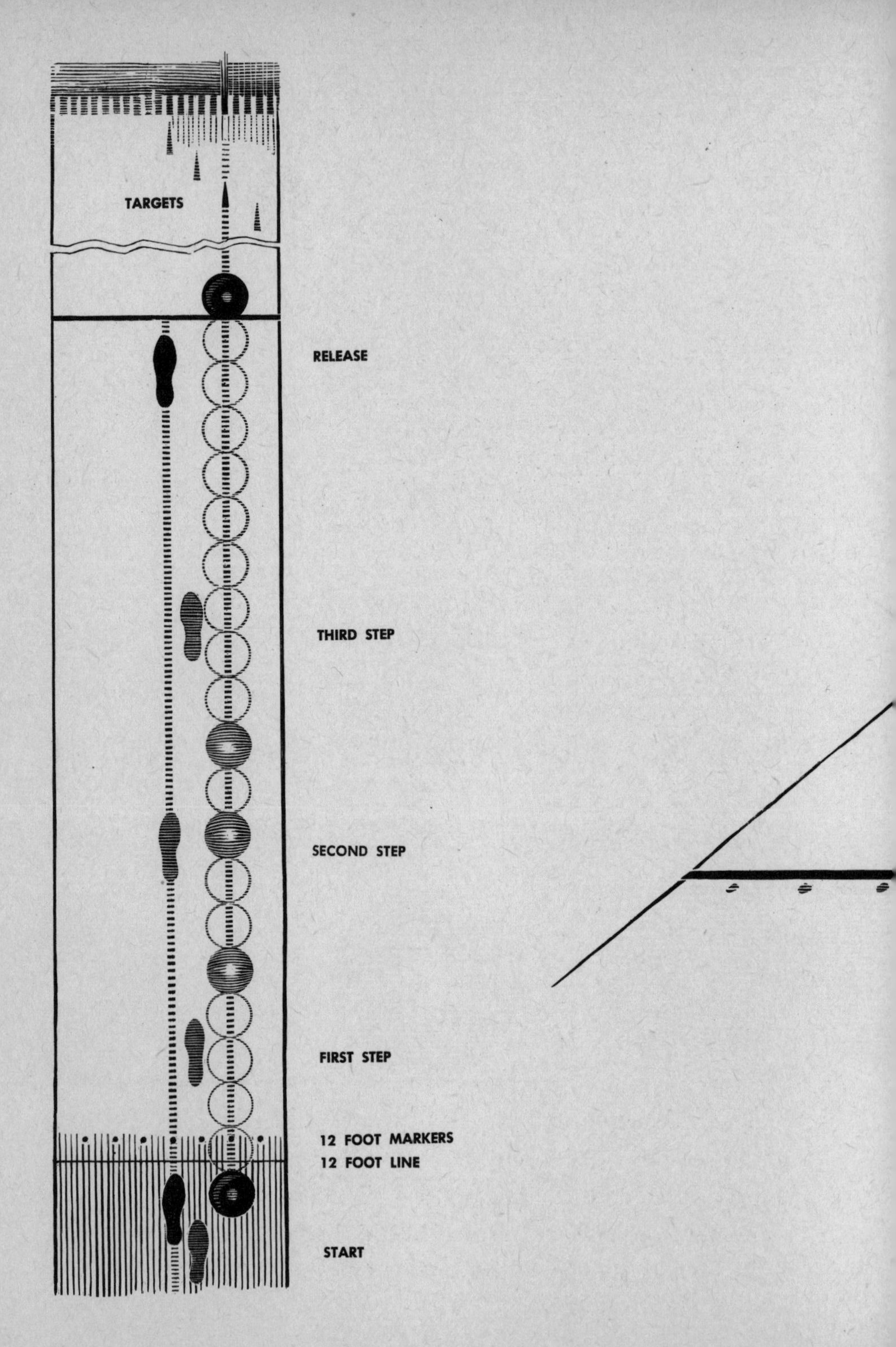
TARGETS
RELEASE
THIRD STEP
SECOND STEP
FIRST STEP
12 FOOT MARKERS
12 FOOT LINE
START

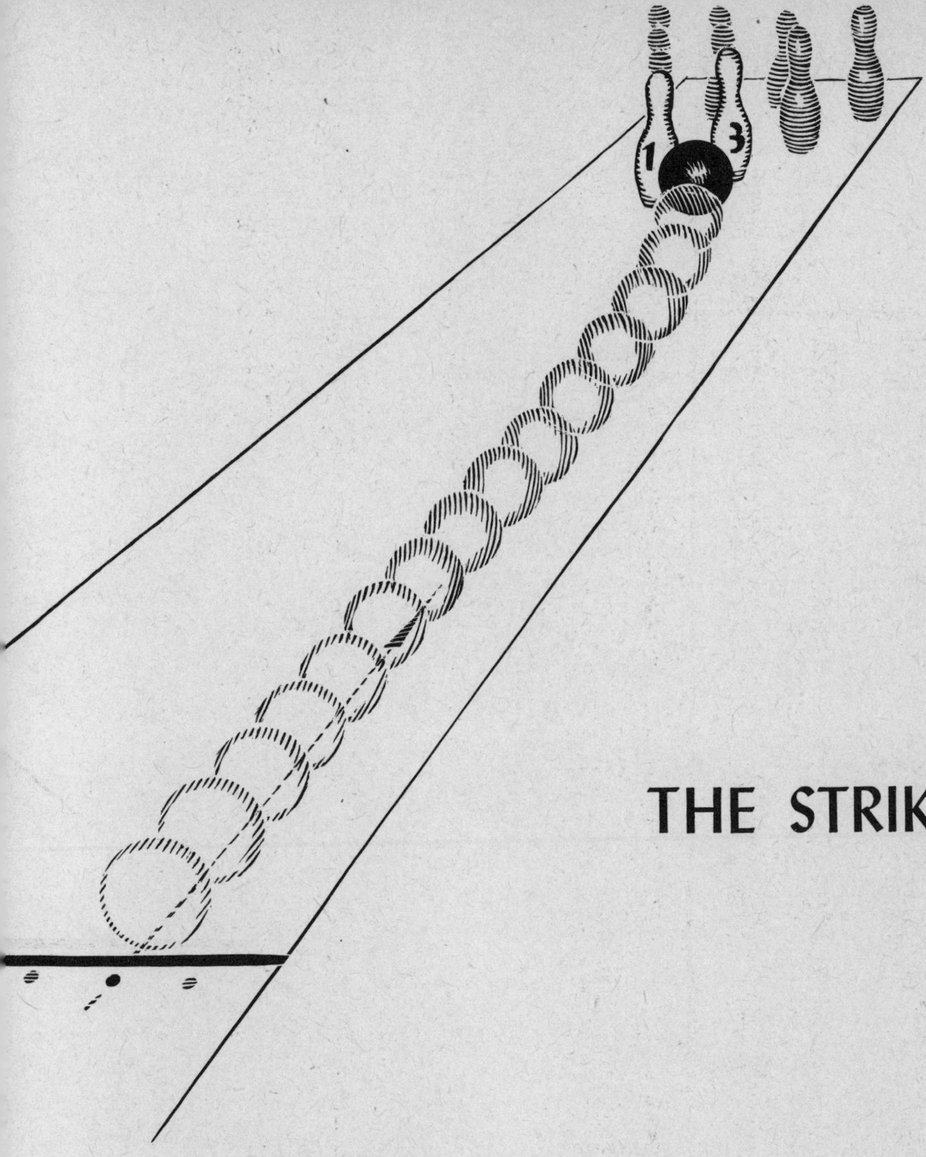

THE STRIKE

All experts agree that the best spot to hit the pins for a strike is between the 1 and 3 pins (or the 1 and 2 pins if the player is left-handed). To do this I release the ball on the floor board that leads directly to the second arrow-shaped marker from the right. The spin on my ball is such that as it nears the pins it will hook slightly to the left to enter the 1-3 pocket.

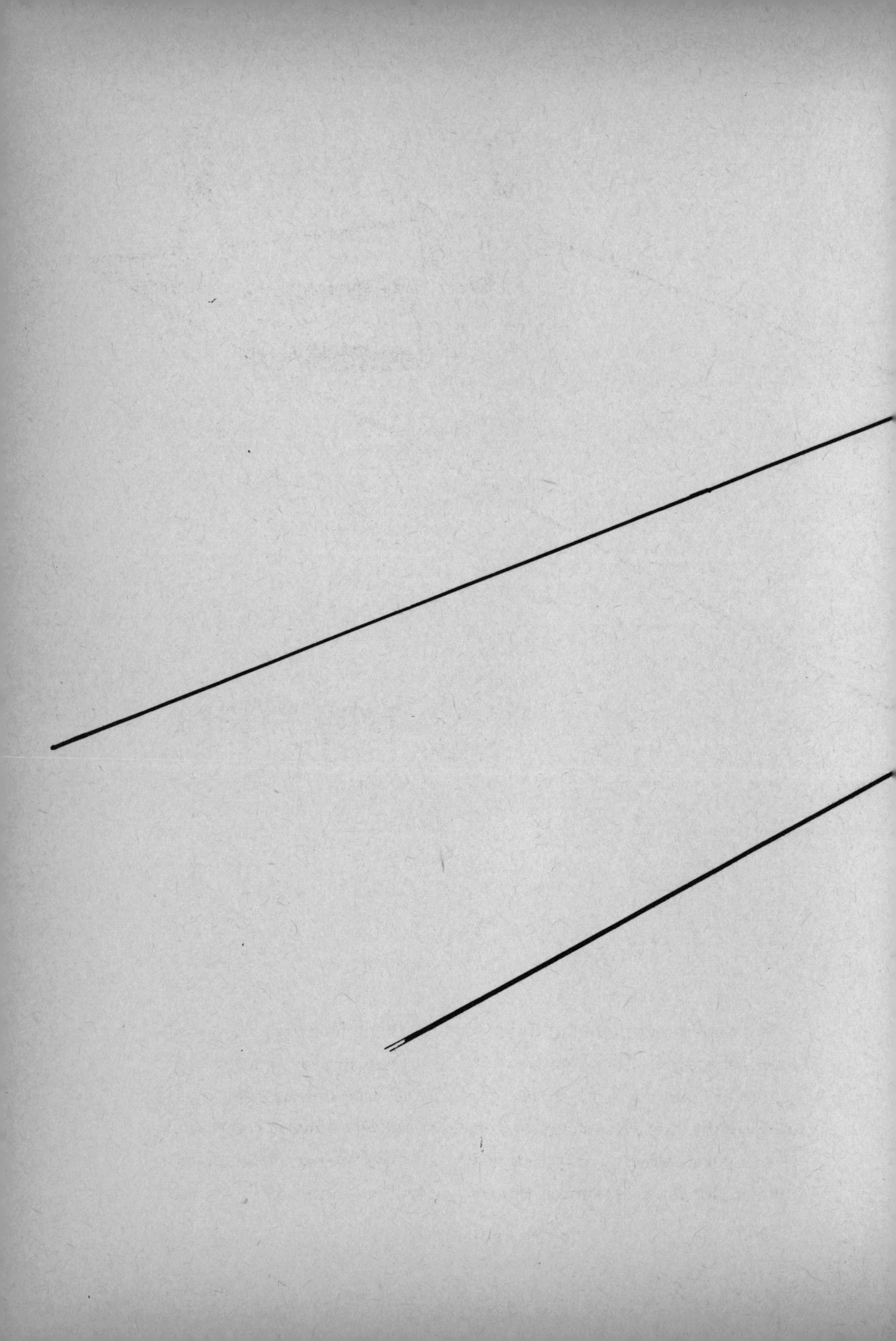

THE SECOND BALL

Many experts recommend different types of delivery for different types of spares—a straight ball for one formation of pins, a reverse hook for another, and so on. I prefer to use exactly the same delivery in all cases, changing only the position where I stand and the target at which I aim. The positions I use may not be the best for you, for they depend on the type of ball you deliver. If it hooks more or less than mine, the best position for you will have to be determined by experiment. The only general rule that applies to all cases is this: you must move your stance to the right when the pins are on the left of the lane, and move left when the pins are on the right.

My first ball is thrown with my shoulders parallel to the foul line at all times. When I throw the second ball I like to imagine a lane that is twisted slightly to the right or left, as shown on the following pages. In this way I can continue to keep my shoulders parallel to the foul line of the *imaginary* lane, and thus execute my delivery exactly as with the first ball.

Though I never look at the pins during the delivery of the first or second ball, for my second, I must of course first glance at the pins to determine their formation and where my imaginary lane will be. Then I take my usual stance, shoulders parallel to the imaginary foul line, while I fix my eyes on wherever my new target happens to be. The pages to follow will make this technique clear with illustrations of the common types of spares and how I set my stance and target for them.

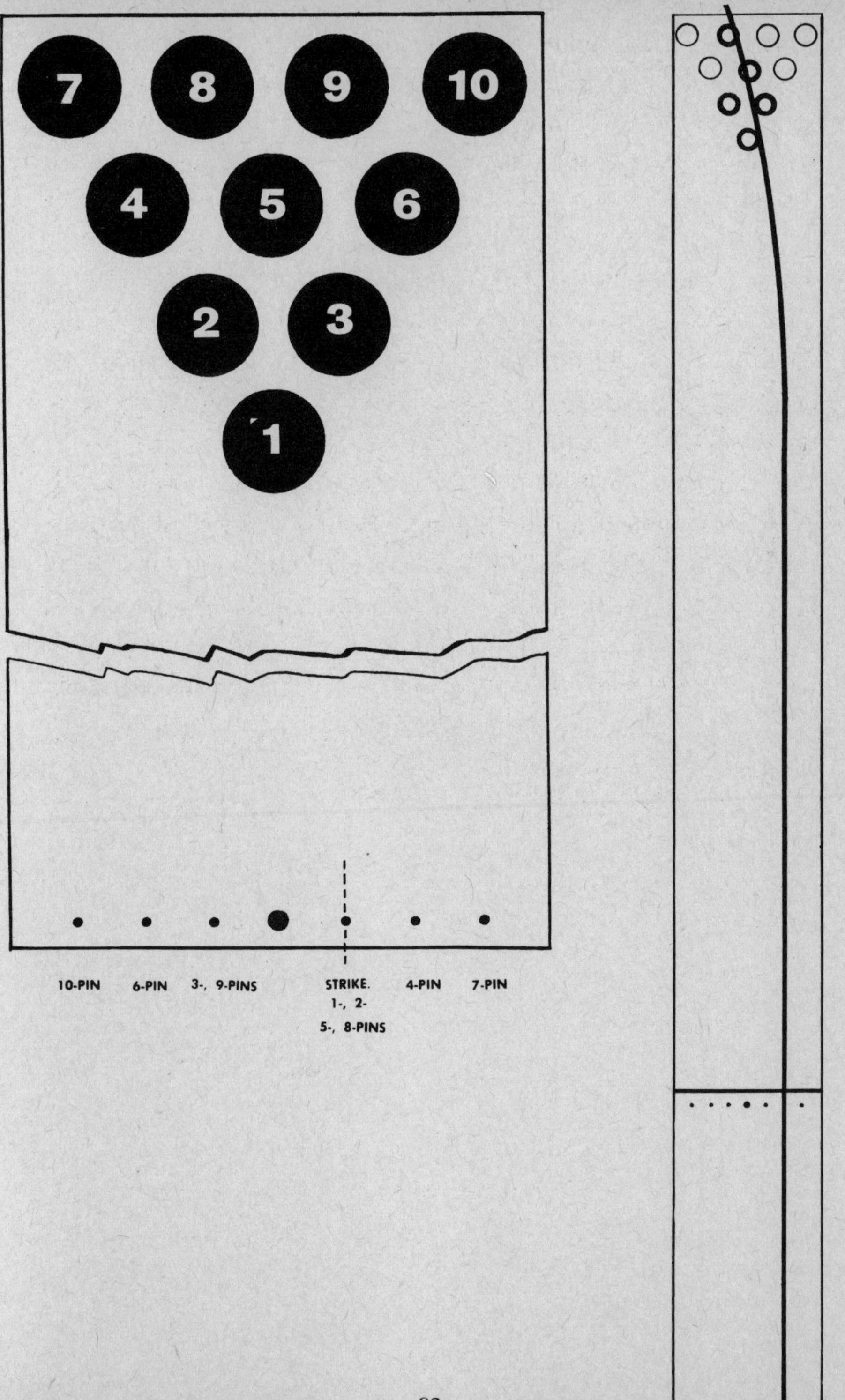
7
8
9
10
4
5
6
2
3
1
10-PIN
6-PIN
3-, 9-PINS
STRIKE.
1-, 2-
5-, 8-PINS
4-PIN
7-PIN

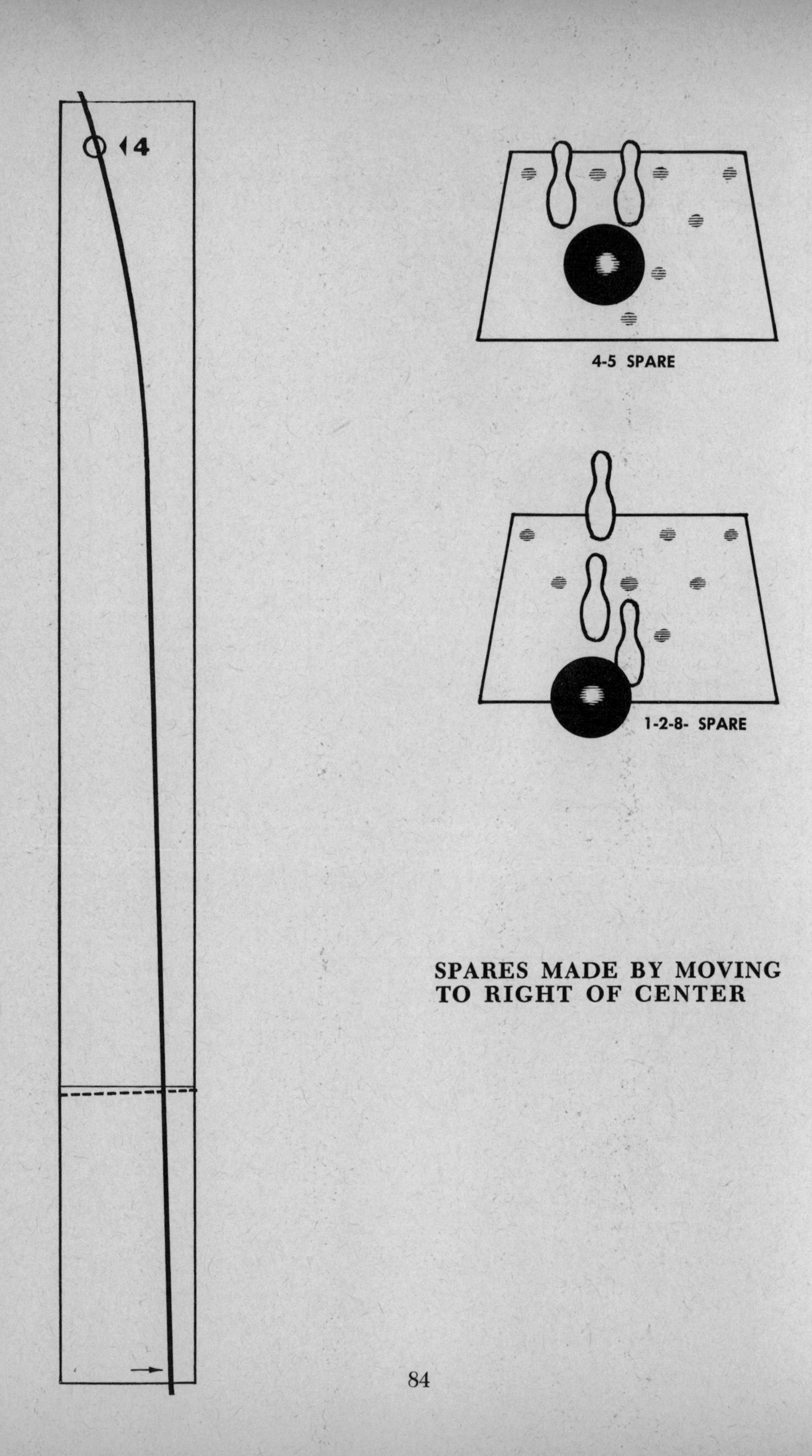

SPARES MADE BY MOVING TO RIGHT OF CENTER

SPARES MADE BY MOVING TO EXTREME RIGHT OF CENTER

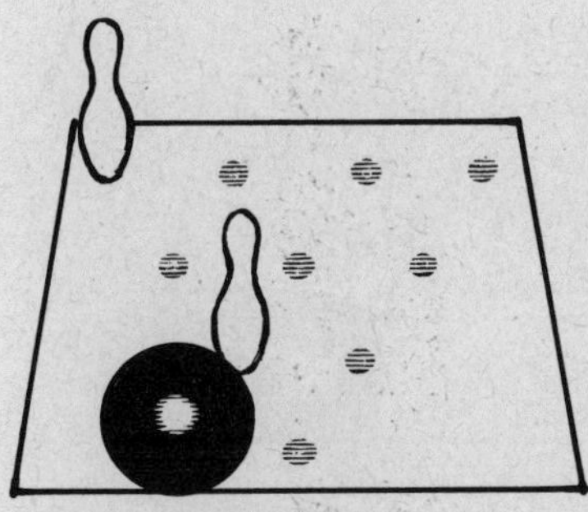

2-7 SPARE

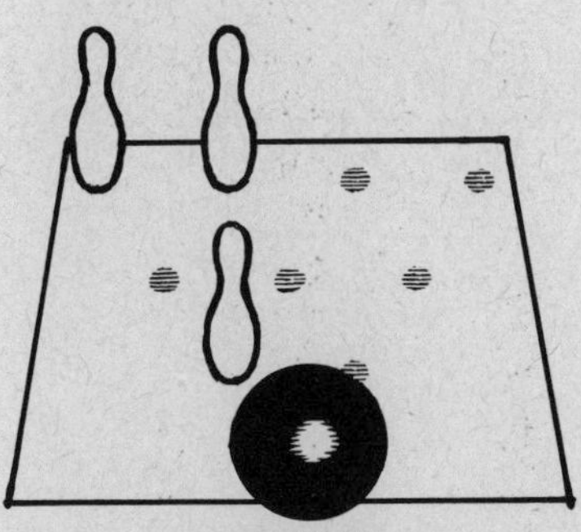

2-7-8 SPARE

7

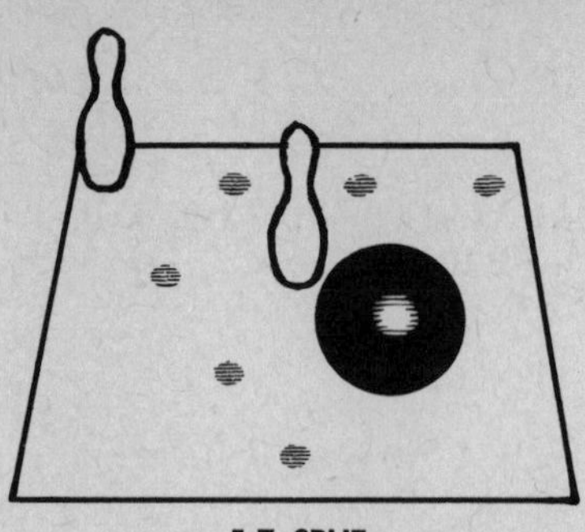

5-7 SPLIT

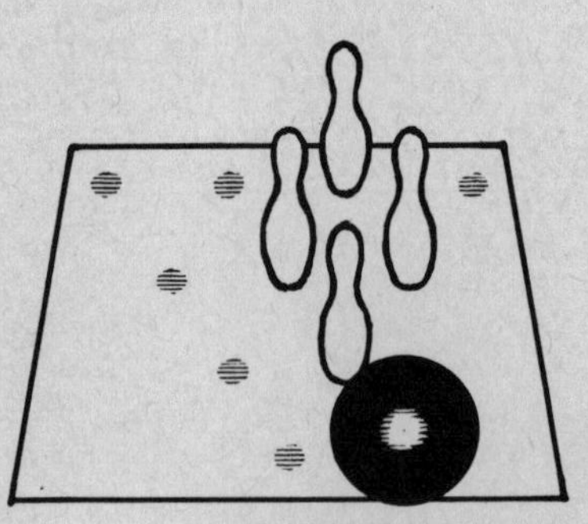

3-5-6-9 SPARE

SPARES MADE BY MOVING TO LEFT OF CENTER

SPARES MADE BY MOVING TO EXTREME LEFT OF CENTER

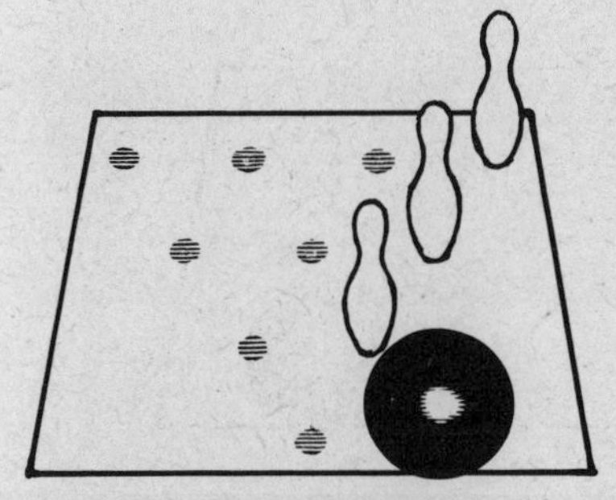

3-6-10 SPARE

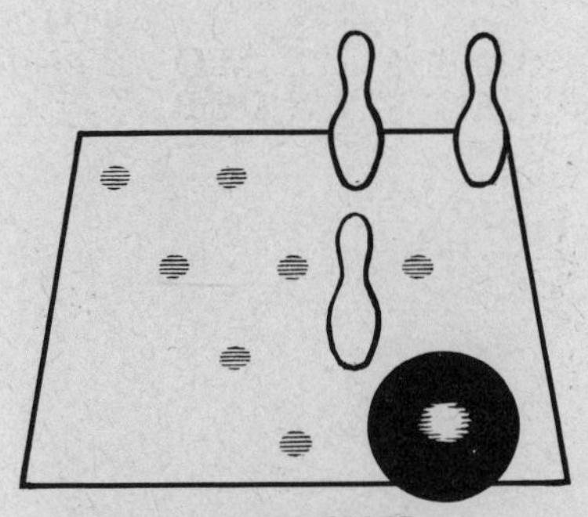

3-9-10 SPARE

Things to Remember

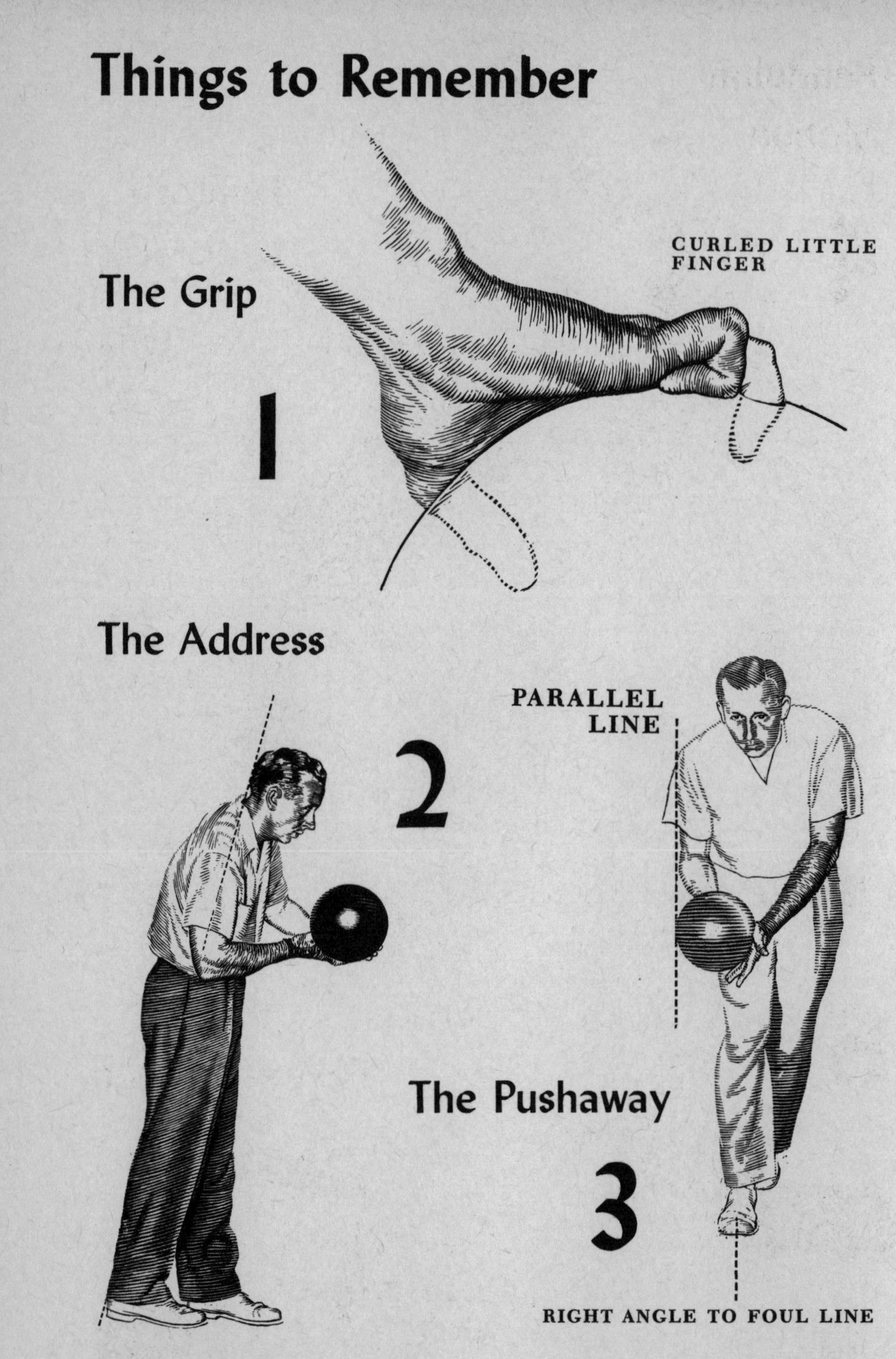

Pendulum
Motion
4
Limit of
Backswing
5
The Release
6
Follow-Through
HEEL STOPS SLIDE

Equipment

In selecting a ball you should pick one that fits comfortably in your hand for the type of grip you use. I have explained earlier how to test for the right size of finger spacing if you adopt my grip on the three-finger ball. Most top bowlers find that they can get a more secure grip on this type of ball, but there is no reason why you shouldn't use the two-finger ball if you really find it easier to handle and are not just trying to prove how strong you are.

Topnotch male bowlers all use a sixteen-pound ball. Most professional women keglers use a fifteen-pounder. The average woman or child, however, as well as men of slight build, will do better with a ball of lighter weight, at least while learning. After you are sure of the type of ball that suits you best, you may wish to buy one of your own. Although all bowling establishments provide balls and shoes, it is difficult to perfect a uniform delivery unless you use the same ball at all times. Owning your own ball is the only way to insure this.

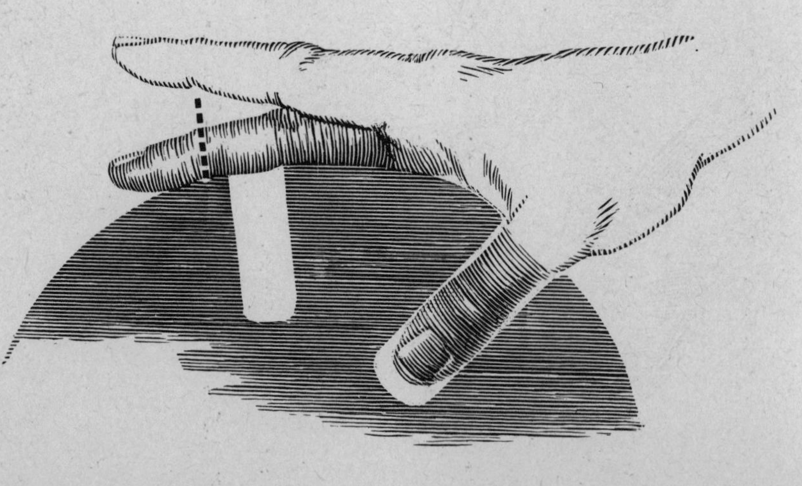

Footwork is sure to suffer if the player's shoes do not fit him comfortably. For this reason I urge all players to own their own bowling shoes. They can now be obtained in a pleasing variety of stylish models and colors. Most manufacturers put a small leather tip on the toe of the rubber-soled right shoe to make the sole last longer at the spot of greatest wear. I always have a shoemaker replace this tip with matching rubber so that I am sure the shoe will keep a firm grip on the lane.

For right-handed bowlers the left shoe has a leather sole for gliding, the right shoe a rubber sole for gripping. This is reversed of course for left-handers.

The player who owns his own bowling ball will need a bag to carry it in. Handsome bags in many different styles and materials are on the market. They zip open easily and most of them have plenty of spare room for bowling shoes and socks. A well-made bag, like the ball it carries, should last a lifetime.

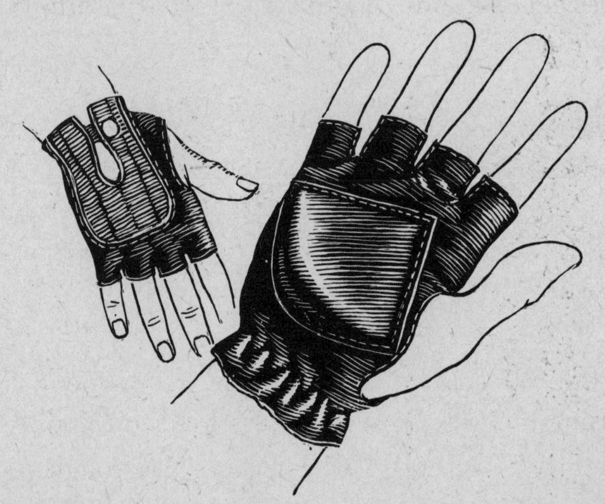

Also I feel it is very important to own your own bowling glove. Many of the professionals, including myself, feel the bowling glove keeps the ball firm in your hand throughout the swing without squeezing; therefore, it eliminates strain on your hand and arm and helps prevent over-turning of the ball which is a common fault of many bowlers.

The Etiquette of Bowling

1. Stay back of the foul line at all times.

2. Your temper and your language should be as controlled as your delivery.

3. Respect the priority of the bowler on the adjoining lane. If he is addressing the pins do not step in front of him to pick your ball off the rack.

4. Stay within the boundaries of your own alley at all times especially when you are applying "body english."

5. Try not to slow up the game. You may get "cold" if there is too long a wait between frames.

6. Resist the temptation of kidding your opponent when he is addressing the pins. You may want the same courtesy when it is your turn to concentrate on making that tough spare.

7. Don't belittle your opponent's victory. Even the champions don't win them all.

8. Don't blame the equipment for splits, misses, and taps. They are all part of the game. You can keep them to a minimum if you set out to correct the faults that cause them.

Tournament Victories and Titles Won by Don Carter

TOURNAMENT VICTORIES

Tournament	*Place*	*Year*
Broad Olympic	Columbus, Ohio	1950
Midway Classic	St. Paul, Minnesota	1951
McMillan Classic	Champaign, Illinois	1951
Skovie's Classic	Chicago, Illinois	1952
Waibel Classic	St. Louis, Missouri	1953
Marino Classic	Milwaukee, Wisconsin	1953
Playdium Classic	East St. Louis, Illinois	1953
Broad Olney Classic	Philadelphia, Pennsylvania	1955
Southside Center	Buffalo, New York	1957
Skovie's Classic	Chicago, Illinois	1958

CHAMPIONSHIPS

PBA National Open Championship – 1960
BPAA All-Star, four times (a record) – 1952, 1953, 1957, 1958.
World's Invitational, five times (a record) – 1957, 1959, 1960, 1961, 1962.
PBA Eastern Open (Paramus, New Jersey) – 1960.
Champions Tournament, inaugural (Madison Square Garden) – 1959.
Southern Match Game – 1957.
BPAA National Team (with Carter Gloves), twice – 1962, 1963.
BPAA National Men's Doubles (with Tom Hennessey) – 1958, 1959.
ABC Classic Team and Team All-Events (with Pfeiffer) – 1953.
ABC Classic Team (with Carter Gloves) – 1962.
National Team Match Game (with Budweiser) – 1956, 1957, 1958, 1959.
Masters Tournament – 1961.
PBA Houston Open – 1962.
PBA Seattle Open – 1962.
PBA Tucson Open – 1962.
PBA Rochester Open – 1962.

Bowler of the Year (BWAA), six times (a record) – 1953, 1954, 1957, 1958, 1960, 1962.

All-American, *Bowlers Journal*, eleven times (all-time record) – 1951, 1952, 1953, 1954, 1957, 1958, 1959, 1960, 1961, 1962, 1963.

All-American, *Bowling Magazine*, eight times (a record) – 1956, 1957, 1958, 1959, 1960, 1961, 1962, 1963.

All-American (various teams) – every year since 1951 (a record).

PBA President three years (a record).

PBA Member of the Year – 1960, 1962 (a record).

Hickok "Bowler of the Decade" Award – 1962.

Won seven live TV matches (National Bowling Champions) in a row in 1956 (a record).

First 800 series on TV (809) on "National Bowling Champions" – 1956.

Highest ABC league average (234) – 1959.

First man to roll three consecutive 1900 series in ABC Tourney – 1951, 1952, 1953.

Record holder for 64-game average in World's Invitational (220) – 1959.

Five consecutive 1800 series in ABC Tournament – 1950–1954.

Member of Budweiser, four-time winner of ABC award for season's high team game.

Member of Ziern Antiques, winner of ABC award for season's high team game.

Fourth highest doubles series in history (1534–756), (Pat Patterson) – 1955.

First to "Make That Spare" on network television.

First to "Make That Spare" twice in a row (a record).

First to crack the jackpot on "Jackpot Bowling" TV show.

Metropolitan (N.Y.) Bowling Writers Award, twice (a record) – 1961, 1963.

Elected to Missouri Hall of Fame – 1962.

Named "Outstanding Athlete in St. Louis" by Elks organization – 1959.

National Bowling Illustrated Bowler of the Year 1962, 1963 (a record).

Honorary Chairman, Australian National All-Star Singles Championship – 1963.

Twenty-three 300 games (thirteen in open play).